First World War
and Army of Occupation
War Diary
France, Belgium and Germany

58 DIVISION
Divisional Troops
Divisional Signal Company
25 January 1917 - 25 June 1919

WO95/2996/8

The Naval & Military Press Ltd
www.nmarchive.com
Published in association with The National Archives

Published by

The Naval & Military Press Ltd

Unit 10 Ridgewood Industrial Park,

Uckfield, East Sussex,

TN22 5QE England

Tel: +44 (0) 1825 749494

www.naval-military-press.com

www.nmarchive.com

This diary has been reprinted in facsimile from the original. Any imperfections are inevitably reproduced and the quality may fall short of modern type and cartographic standards.

Contents

Document type	Place/Title	Date From	Date To
Heading	WO95/2996/8		
Heading	War Diary Of 58th Divisional Signal Coy. R.E From Jan 25th 1917 To February 26th 1917 (Volume I)		
War Diary	Havre	25/01/1917	26/01/1917
War Diary	Frevent	27/01/1917	27/01/1917
War Diary	Frohen-Le-Grand	28/01/1917	06/02/1917
War Diary	Lucheux	06/02/1917	20/02/1917
War Diary	Henu	20/02/1917	26/02/1917
Operation(al) Order(s)	58th Divisional Order No. 2	05/02/1917	05/02/1917
Miscellaneous	March Table for Tuesday		
Operation(al) Order(s)	Company Order No. 2	20/02/1917	20/02/1917
Operation(al) Order(s)	Company Order No. 1		
Heading	War Diary Of 58th Divisional Signal Coy. R.E From Feb 27th 1917 To March 26th 1917 (Volume I)		
War Diary	Henu	27/02/1917	01/03/1917
War Diary	Bavincourt	01/03/1917	29/03/1917
War Diary	Lucheux	29/03/1917	01/04/1917
War Diary	Frohen-Le-Grand	01/04/1917	05/04/1917
War Diary	Bus-Les-Artois	06/04/1917	17/04/1917
War Diary	Bihucourt	17/04/1917	16/05/1917
War Diary	Mory	17/05/1917	24/06/1917
War Diary	Courcelles	24/06/1917	29/06/1917
Operation(al) Order(s)	Operation Order No. 8	28/03/1917	28/03/1917
Operation(al) Order(s)	Operation Order No. 9	31/03/1917	31/03/1917
Operation(al) Order(s)	Operation Order No. 10	04/04/1917	04/04/1917
Diagram etc	Diagram		
Operation(al) Order(s)	Order No. 12	16/06/1917	16/06/1917
Operation(al) Order(s)	58th Divisional Signal Co.R.E. Signal Order No. 13	22/06/1917	22/06/1917
War Diary	Courcelles	01/07/1917	10/07/1917
War Diary	Ytres	11/07/1917	31/07/1917
War Diary	Fosseux	01/08/1917	01/08/1917
Operation(al) Order(s)	Signal Order No. 15	23/07/1917	23/07/1917
War Diary	Fosseux	01/08/1917	25/08/1917
War Diary	A16 C 2.3 ("X" Camp) Sheet 28	26/08/1917	29/08/1917
Miscellaneous	Order For Move Of N.2 And N.1 Section From Fosseux	24/08/1917	24/08/1917
Operation(al) Order(s)	Signal Order No. 16	28/08/1917	28/08/1917
War Diary	C Camp A30d00 Sheet 28	04/09/1917	19/09/1917
War Diary	Canal Bank C 25d3.3	20/09/1917	28/09/1917
War Diary	Browne Camp	29/09/1917	29/09/1917
War Diary	Zutkerque	30/09/1917	30/09/1917
Operation(al) Order(s)	Signal Order No. 17	10/09/1917	10/09/1917
Map	Map		
War Diary	Zutkerque	01/10/1917	20/10/1917
War Diary	Poperinghe	22/10/1917	24/10/1917
War Diary	Canal Bank C 19 C 3.2	25/10/1917	17/11/1917
War Diary	Proven	17/11/1917	27/11/1917
War Diary	Nielles Les Blequin	04/12/1917	09/12/1917
War Diary	Canal Bank C 19 C 3.2	09/12/1917	09/01/1918
War Diary	Couthove Chau	15/01/1918	20/01/1918

War Diary	Corbie	21/01/1918	07/02/1918
War Diary	Rouez	09/02/1918	27/02/1918
War Diary	Quierzy	03/03/1918	24/03/1918
War Diary	Varennes	24/03/1918	24/03/1918
War Diary	Camelin	24/03/1918	27/03/1918
War Diary	Blerancourt	27/03/1918	31/03/1918
Heading	War Diary 58th Divisional Signal Company R.E April 1918		
War Diary	Blerancourt	01/04/1918	05/04/1918
War Diary	Glisy	05/04/1918	13/04/1918
War Diary	Fort Manoir Chateau	13/04/1918	28/04/1918
War Diary	St Ricquier	28/04/1918	07/05/1918
War Diary	Molliens-Au-Bois	08/05/1918	17/05/1918
War Diary	Contay	17/05/1918	02/06/1918
War Diary	Molliens-Au-Bois	03/06/1918	10/06/1918
War Diary	Cavillon	14/06/1918	20/06/1918
War Diary	Beaucourt	23/06/1918	30/06/1918
Miscellaneous	Destructions Of Telegraph And Telephone Routes	22/09/1918	22/09/1918
War Diary	Beaucourt	01/07/1918	31/07/1918
Heading	58th Divl. Engineers 58th Divisional Signal Company Royal Engineers August 1918		
Miscellaneous	This War Diary Refers To 58th Divsl. Signal Company	25/09/1918	25/09/1918
Miscellaneous	H.Q. 58th Division	22/09/1918	22/09/1918
War Diary	Beaucourt	01/08/1918	04/08/1918
War Diary	Querrieu	04/08/1918	07/08/1918
War Diary	G 19c3.5	08/08/1918	13/08/1918
War Diary	St. Gratien	14/08/1918	31/08/1918
War Diary	Maricourt A 19b 5.2	01/09/1918	06/09/1918
War Diary	Bouchavesnes C 20b 3.1	07/09/1918	07/09/1918
War Diary	Gurlu Wood D 22 A 24	08/09/1918	26/09/1918
War Diary	Fillers Chatel	27/09/1918	29/09/1918
War Diary	Sains-En-Gohelle	30/09/1918	30/09/1918
Diagram etc	Route Diagram		
War Diary	Sains-En-Gohelle	01/10/1918	12/10/1918
War Diary	Fosse 11	13/10/1918	16/10/1918
War Diary	Montigny	17/10/1918	18/10/1918
War Diary	Moncheaux Bersee	19/10/1918	20/10/1918
War Diary	Mouchin	21/10/1918	31/10/1918
Miscellaneous	G.S 3550	13/10/1918	13/10/1918
Miscellaneous	58th (London) Division 58th Divn. G.S 8/159	19/10/1918	19/10/1918
War Diary	Mouchin	01/11/1918	08/11/1918
War Diary	Bleharies	09/11/1918	09/11/1918
War Diary	Wiers	10/11/1918	10/11/1918
War Diary	Beloeil	11/11/1918	28/11/1918
War Diary	Peruwelz	01/12/1918	24/12/1918
War Diary	Peruwelz	01/12/1918	31/12/1918
War Diary	Peruwelz	01/01/1919	31/01/1919
War Diary	Peruwelz	01/02/1919	28/02/1919
War Diary	Peruwelz	01/03/1919	19/03/1919
War Diary	Lenge	19/03/1919	25/06/1919

58

Vol 192

Confidential.

War Diary of

58th Divisional Signal Coy R. E.

From Jan. 25th 1917 To February 26th 1917.

(Volume I)

Instructions regarding War Diaries and Intelligence Summaries are contained in F. S. Regs., Part II. and the Staff Manual respectively. Title Pages will be prepared in manuscript.

WAR DIARY
or
~~INTELLIGENCE SUMMARY~~
(Erase heading not required.)

Army Form C. 2118.

Place	Date	Hour	Summary of Events and Information	Remarks and references to Appendices
HAVRE	25-1-17	1-0pm	H. Q. and No. 1. Sections of Unit disembarked ex S.S. "NORTHWESTERN MILLER" at BOOTH LINE QUAY.	
"	25-1-17	4-30pm	Departed from Quay to march to Rest Camp.	
"	25-1-17	6-0pm	Arrived at No. 2 REST CAMP, HAVRE. Wagons parked, horses picketed, and troops accommodated under canvas.	
"	26-1-17	11'15am	Departed from Rest Camp, marched to entraining Depot HAVRE.	W.G.[illegible]
"	26-1-17	12'30pm	Arrived ENTRAINING DEPOT, HAVRE, loaded wagons, & horses and entrained.	
"	26-1-17	3'40pm	Train left HAVRE.	
"	26-1-17	11'10am	Motor-cyclists and Mechanical Transport departed from No. 2 REST CAMP HAVRE to proceed by road to FROHEN-LE-GRAND via ABBEVILLE, under 2/LT. G.D. ARDEN.	
FREVENT	27-1-17	7'40pm	Train arrived at FREVENT, and transport & personnel detrained.	
FREVENT	27-1-17	10'10pm	Departed from FREVENT and marched to FROHEN-LE-GRAND.	W.G.[illegible]
FROHEN-LE-GRAND	28-1-17	1'25am	Arrived at FROHEN-LE-GRAND. Horses picketed & wagons parked. Troops billetted in barn	
"	28-1-17	5-15pm	Motor-cyclists and Mechanical Transport arrived at FROHEN-LE-GRAND.	
"	28-1-17	9'30am	Signal Office opened at the CHATEAU, FROHEN-LE-GRAND. Telephone line to DOULLENS Exchange manned.	
"	29-1-17	12 noon	Letter service commenced to 173rd and 174th BDES. at IVERGNY and BACHIMONT respectively.	W.G.[illegible]
"	29-1-17	2pm	Visited A.D.S. XVIII. CORPS reference communications. Division not yet definitely allotted to any Corps: no arrangements possible.	W.G.[illegible]

2449 Wt. W14957/M90 750,000 1/16 J.B.C. & A. Forms/C.2118/12.

Army Form C. 2118.

WAR DIARY
or
~~INTELLIGENCE SUMMARY~~
(Erase heading not required.)

Instructions regarding War Diaries and Intelligence Summaries are contained in F. S. Regs., Part II. and the Staff Manual respectively. Title Pages will be prepared in manuscript.

Place	Date	Hour	Summary of Events and Information	Remarks and references to Appendices
FROHEN-LE-GRAND	30/1/17	11 am	Attended conference with A.D.S. XVIII Corps, O.C. Signals 46th + 49th Divisions.	
"	"	3 pm	Returned. 58th Division definitely allotted to XVIII. Corps.	
"	31/1/17	10'15 am	Telephone line to ~~[illegible]~~ DOULLENS Exchange plugged through to 18th CORPS at PAS, Sounders superimposed; signals good.	[initials]
"	4/2/17	6'30 pm	Received information from General Staff Divisional H.Q. moving to LUCHEUX 6th inst.	
	4/2/17	9'0 am	No. 4 Section disembarked at HAVRE	
"	5/2/17	11 am	Visited O.C. SIGNALS 30th DIV. LUCHEUX and arranged for taking over communications. Returned 3'30 pm.	[initials]
"	"	2'45 pm	Advance party under 2/LT. ARDEN, G.D., left FROHEN-LE-GRAND for LUCHEUX to establish Signal Office.	
"	"			
FROHEN-LE-GRAND	5-2-17.	2'50 pm	Received Divisional Secret Memo. "Order No. 2, Copy No. 8" ordering move, together with March Table. [initials]	Appx. A.
"	6-2-17	10 am	Departed from FROHEN-LE-GRAND and marched via DOULLENS - BOUT - DES PRES to LUCHEUX.	
LUCHEUX	6-2-17.	2'55 pm	Arrived LUCHEUX.	
"	6-2-17	12 noon	DHQ Signal Office closed at FROHEN-LE-GRAND, and opened at LUCHEUX same hour. 173rd BDE at IVERGNY, 174th BDE at POMMERA	
"	6-2-17.		HQ 175th BDE. and No. 4 SECTION arrived at REMAISNIL.	
"	7-2-17		Took over a metallic line from LUCHEUX to SUS-ST-LÉGER and extended same to 173rd BDE at IVERGNY, working to 174th BDE. on earth return circuit. [initials]	

2449 Wt. W14957/M90 750,000 1/16 J.B.C. & A. Forms/C.2118/12.

Army Form C. 2118.

Instructions regarding War Diaries and Intelligence Summaries are contained in F. S. Regs., Part II. and the Staff Manual respectively. Title Pages will be prepared in manuscript.

WAR DIARY
or
INTELLIGENCE SUMMARY

(Erase heading not required.)

Place	Date	Hour	Summary of Events and Information	Remarks and references to Appendices
LUCHEUX	7-2-17	3 pm	175th BDE. HQ moved from REMAISNIL to LE SOUICH. Working on phone and sounder with sounder superimposed	
"	8-2-17	10.30 am	2/LT. ARDEN G.D. leaves unit for attachment to 46th DIVN. at HENU.	
"	"	9 am	K. Cable Det. leaves to lay second leg of metallic circuit to 174th BDE to POMMERA	
"	"	12.15 pm	Received orders from G. Staff that No. 3 Section will be attached to 139 INF. BDE. HQ. at SOUASTRE from 9th–14th. insts and No. 2 Section to 148th INF. BDE. HQ. at LA CAUCHIE from 11–16th insts. Signal Officers informed accordingly.	
"	"	2.45 pm	Through to 173rd BDE. on phone with sounder superimposed. Signals good.	
"	"	4 pm	Line to 174th BDE completed by K. Det.	
"	"	5 pm	Information received from G. Staff that attachment of No. 3. Section would commence 10th inst. instead of 9th.	
"	9-2-17	10 am	Through to 174th BDE by 'phone with sounder superimposed. Signals good.	
"	"	3 pm	Telephone installed at 58th Supply Column. Speaking good.	
"	10-2-17	10 am	Twelve Cyclist Orderlies report from Inf. Bdes. for duty with Unit as D.Rs.	
"	"	"	Six linemen leave No. 1 Section for attachment to 46th DIVN. at HENU.	
"	"	"	No. 3. Section leave POMMERA for attachment to 139th. INF. BDE. HQ. at SOUASTRE	
"	11-2-17	10 am	No. 2 Section leave IVERGNY for 148th. INF. BDE. HQ at LA CAUCHIE.	
"	"	10.25 am	Four N.C.Os. and five men left LUCHEUX for attachment to 49th DIVSL. SIGNALS RE at BAVINCOURT.	

2449 Wt. W14957/M90 750,000 1/16 J.B.C. & A. Forms/C.2118/12.

Army Form C. 2118.

WAR DIARY
or
~~INTELLIGENCE SUMMARY~~

(Erase heading not required.)

Instructions regarding War Diaries and Intelligence Summaries are contained in F. S. Regs., Part II. and the Staff Manual respectively. Title Pages will be prepared in manuscript.

Place	Date	Hour	Summary of Events and Information	Remarks and references to Appendices
LUCHEUX	11/2/17	2'30pm	Visited Signals 49th Divn. returning at 6 pm. with diagram of Divisional lines.	
"	"	6'50pm	Twelve cyclists reported from XVIII. CORPS CYCLIST BATTN. for permanent attachment.	
"	12/2/17	9'30am	Twelve Inf. Orderlies returned to their respective Units; transported by lorry as far as their Bde. H.Q.	
"	12/2/17	9am	Visited Signals 49th DIVN also inspecting Signal Offices of three INF. BDES, returning at 6pm.	
"	13/2/17	10 am	Visited 175th INF. BDE. to arrange with Bde. Staff for attachment of Signal Section to 147th INF. BDE.	
"	"	9'15am	LIEUT. E.W. GILL visits Sigs. 46th DIV. ARTY. returning 1'30 pm.	
"	"	1'30pm	2/LT. G.D ARDEN returns from attachment to 46th DIVN.	
"	"	2'45pm	P.E.L. Car and lorry arrived.	
"	14/2/17	8'45pm	2/LT. S.G. BEAZLEY reports for duty as "X" Establishment Officer	
"	15/2/17	8'20am	Lorry despatched to SOUASTRE. LIEUT. HENRY and nine other ranks conveyed to BAILLEULMONT for attachment to 146th BDE, remainder of section returning to H.Q. 174th BDE at POMMERA.	
"	"	4pm	LIEUT. J.S.W. STONE reports for duty as Officer i/c Signals 173rd BDE.	
"	14/2/17	2pm	2/LT. BRYANT Sigs. 175th BDE and eight other ranks attached to 148th INF. BDE.	
"	"	"	No. 2 Section returned from 148th BDE. to IVERGNY.	
"	"	"	Capt. BATESON attached to Sigs. 49th DIVN.	

2449 Wt. W14957/M90 750,000 1/16 J.B.C. & A. Forms/C.2118/12.

Army Form C. 2118.

Instructions regarding War Diaries and Intelligence Summaries are contained in F. S. Regs., Part II. and the Staff Manual respectively. Title Pages will be prepared in manuscript.

WAR DIARY
or
INTELLIGENCE SUMMARY
(Erase heading not required.)

Place	Date	Hour	Summary of Events and Information	Remarks and references to Appendices
LUCHEUX	16/2/17	8'30am	LIEUT. E.W. GILL attached to SIGS. 49TH DIV. ARTY.	
"	"	"	Electrician sent to 49TH DIVN. to inspect civilian electric light plant.	
"	"	"	C.S.M. MORRIS visits billets at 49TH. DIV. returning same evening.	
"	"	10'30am	Visited 173rd. BDE. with LIEUT. J.S.W. STONE & handed over sectional stores.	
"	"	2'30pm	Visited 46th. DIVN. to arrange details of taking over. Proceeded to POMMIER and inspected main buny. ~~[illegible]~~. Proceeded to BAVINCOURT arriving 5-30 pm. to arrange details of taking over, returning 7 pm. [signature]	
"	15/2/17	5'30pm	Visited A.D.S. XVIII. CORPS and discussed question of Area stores and handing over of buzzing Units, returning 7'15 pm.	
"	17/2/17	9-30am	Four pioneers of No. 4 Section despatched for attachment to 148TH. BDE.	
			2-LT. BRYANT returns to 175TH. BDE at LE SOUICH	
"	"	11am	Received 58th DIVSL. Operation Order No. 3.	
"	18/2/17.	9am	Cable Det. leaves and reels up cable line from IVERGNY to LE SOUICH [signature]	
"	"	9'5am	Received orders all lorries off owing to thaw.	
"	"	"	1 Cpl. 2 ORs. despatched to 49th DIVN. preparatory to taking over.	
"	"	10am.	Proceeded by car to 49th DIVN. BAVINCOURT to conference as to routes on taking over the front.	
"	"	3 pm	Capt. BATESON and LT. GILL returned to LUCHEUX, LIEUT. HENRY ~~at~~ POMMERA on completion of attachment to 49th DIVSL. SIGS. and 146th. BDE. SIGS. respectively.	
"	"	6pm	Following subscribers disconnected from Divisl. Telephone Exchange — Camp Comdt., C.R.E.	[signature]

2449 Wt. W14957/M90 750,000 1/16 J.B.C. & A. Forms/C.2118/12.

Army Form C. 2118.

WAR DIARY
or
INTELLIGENCE SUMMARY
(Erase heading not required.)

Instructions regarding War Diaries and Intelligence Summaries are contained in F. S. Regs., Part II. and the Staff Manual respectively. Title Pages will be prepared in manuscript.

Place	Date	Hour	Summary of Events and Information	Remarks and references to Appendices
LUCHEUX	18/2/17	6 pm (contd)	30th DIVSL. DEPOT; 58TH DIVSL. SUPPLY. COL., A.D.M.S., A.P.M.,	
"	"	7'15 pm	Received 58th Divsl. Operation Order No. 4. and acknowledged same.	
"	"	7'15 pm	Received 'phone message from "G" Staff warning alteration in disposition of Artillery H.Q. on taking over front.	
"	"	10 pm	10-line cordless exchange inserted at LUCHEUX Office and 20-line extracted.	
"	19/2/17	9 am	2/LT. ARDEN and five O.R. left with instruments etc. for HENU to take over Divsl. Office. [initials]	
"	"	9'15 am	Conference with CRA 58th DIVN. as to positions of R.A. H.Q. and disposition of Artillery BDES. on the new front.	
"	"	2'15 pm	Visited 46th. Division to see that instruments and new H.Q. were in order and arranged final details of taking over, returning 4 pm.	
"	"	2'15 pm	Received C.R.A. Divisional Operation Order No. 2.	
"	"	6'30 pm	Arranged with Corps Signal Officer over the 'phone for direct line 27 A and B from POMMERA to be plugged through PAS on to HENU Exchange.	
"	"	6'40 pm	Conversation on 'phone with O.C. 46th. Sigs. Details of handing over exchanges arranged.	
"	"	7 pm	Company Orders Nos 1 and 2 (copies attached) issued to H.Q. and Bde. Sections.	"B"
"	20/2/17	10 am	Column left LUCHEUX and proceeded to HENU via PAS arriving 2 pm. [signature]	
"	"	10 am	Two Cable Dets. left LUCHEUX to reel up lines LUCHEX — POMMERA, proceeding thence to HENU, arriving 3-30 pm.	

2449 Wt. W14957/M90 750,000 1/16 J.B.C. & A. Forms/C.2118/12.

Instructions regarding War Diaries and Intelligence Summaries are contained in F. S. Regs., Part II. and the Staff Manual respectively. Title Pages will be prepared in manuscript.

WAR DIARY
or
INTELLIGENCE SUMMARY
(Erase heading not required.)

Army Form C. 2118.

Place	Date	Hour	Summary of Events and Information	Remarks and references to Appendices
HENU	20/2/17	10 am	Divisional Office opened. Through to 187th Bde. POMMERA and 138th Bde. SOUASTRE.	
"	"	10 am	173rd Bde. Sig. Office closed at IVERGNY. No. 2 Bde. Sec. proceeded to SOUASTRE and re-opened there at 5'15 pm.	
"	21/2/17	9am	Double comic airline laid from ST. AMAND dugout to D pole.	
"	"	10am	Signal Office 175th Bde. closed at LE SOUICH. No 4 Section proceeded to POMMERA. Office opened at POMMERA at same hour.	
"	"	10am	Signal Office 174th Bde. closed at POMMERA. No. 3 Section proceeded to BAILLEULMONT and re-opened there at 11'15 am.	
"	"	10'30am	Visited LA CAUCHIE Exchange and 49th. Signals BAVINCOURT	
"	"	4-0pm	Electric light lorry arrived HENU from LUCHEUX. Lights installed and working at 6 pm.	
"	"	2-0pm	58th. Divl. Operation Order received and acknowledged.	
"	"	10-0pm	Electric light out. Lighting set seized owing to thick oil.	
"	"	12mdnt.	Lighting set bearings cleared, but engine not re-started.	
"	22/2/17	9 am	Capt. Bateson and 4 linemen tested routes at ST. AMAND & SOUASTRE up to A pole, returning 7 p.m.	
"	"	9'45am	Wagon leaves for LUCHEUX to issue Buzzer Units to R.A. Bdes. Test panels etc issued to No. 3 Section.	
"	"	10 am	Visited ST. AMAND, A pole, Souastre and S pole returning 1'15 pm.	
"	"	5 pm	Electric lighting set again in order and running well.	
"	"	5'15pm	Second sounder line (superimposed) through to XVIII Corps.	

2449 Wt. W14957/M90 750,000 1/16 J.B.C. & A. Forms/C.2118/12.

Army Form C. 2118.

Instructions regarding War Diaries and Intelligence Summaries are contained in F. S. Regs., Part II. and the Staff Manual respectively. Title Pages will be prepared in manuscript.

WAR DIARY
or
INTELLIGENCE SUMMARY
(Erase heading not required.)

Place	Date	Hour	Summary of Events and Information	Remarks and references to Appendices
HENU	23/2/17	9'30am	Working at "A" pole till 1 pm. Lines tested through and found O.K. less G.K. 20. Comic pair laid from ST. AMAND to D pole. GK22 led in by D5. from SOUASTRE pole to 138 BDE Signal Office.	
"	"	2pm	At H pole. Lines tested.	
"	"	4pm	LUCHEUX telephone exchange taken over by 49th Divl. Signals. D.A.D.O.S. disconnected.	
"	"	4pm	A.D.A.S. XVIII. Corps inspects Signal Office.	
"	"	12'15pm	58th Divl. Operation Order No. 7. received and acknowledged.	
"	"	9'30pm	" " " " 8 " " —"—	
"	"	10pm	Received authority (Wire Q570) from H.Q. 58th Divn. for movement of 2 lorries LUCHEUX to HENU.	
"	24/2/17	9am	Linemen despatched to 173rd Bde (SPR. BEALEY. A.) and 174th Bde. (SPR. LYNELEY. A.J.)	[initials]
"	"	"	CPL. CAMPBELL and 3 linemen despatched for duty to LA CAUCHIE EXCHANGE.	
"	"	9am—4pm	Ten cyclist orderlies report from 173rd 174th and 175th Bdes. for duty.	
"	"	2pm.	30-cwt. lorry and 3-ton lorry arrived HENU.	
"	"	11'30pm	Received wire G193 from G. Staff. Instructions to be ready to move at short notice.	
"	25/2/17	7'30am	2/Cpl PUGH and two Telephone Operators despatched to LA CAUCHIE Exchange for duty	
"	"	8'0am	Divisional instns. to be ready to move cancelled by G. Staff wire G199.	[initials]
"	"	2pm.	173rd Bde. took over front of 148th Bde. Relief of Signals already completed by No. 2 Section at 11 am.	

2449 Wt. W14957/M90 750,000 1/16 J.B.C. & A. Forms/C.2118/12.

Army Form C. 2118.

Instructions regarding War Diaries and Intelligence Summaries are contained in F. S. Regs., Part II. and the Staff Manual respectively. Title Pages will be prepared in manuscript.

WAR DIARY
or
INTELLIGENCE SUMMARY

(Erase heading not required.)

Place	Date	Hour	Summary of Events and Information	Remarks and references to Appendices
HENU	25/2/17	11pm	Contact on main telephone lines to LA CAUCHIE and POMMIER. Out testing for fault till 3 am. [initials]	
"	26/2/17	9'30am	Fault cleared.	
"	"	9'0am	2/LT. BEAZLEY stationed at LA CAUCHIE in charge of Northern Area.	
"	"	10'0am	LA CAUCHIE Telephone Exchange in good working order.	
"	"	10'0am	Four motor-cyclists reported for duty from XVIII. Corps.	
"	"	10'0am	Relief of 49th DIVN. effected. Direct Sounder lines to 137th., 138th., 147th., 173rd. and 174th. Bdes. and XVIII Corps.	
"	"	3'30pm	Sounder line through to 147th Bde.	
"	"	2'30pm	Divisional Train on 137th Bde. Exchange.	
"	"	2-0pm	Twelve Cyclists belonging to XVIII. Corps Cyclist Battn. return to their Unit.	
"	"			

W G Michelmore
Captain RE
Comdg Signals. 58 Division
27/2/16.

2449 Wt. W14957/M90 750,000 1/16 J.B.C. & A. Forms/C.2118/12.

APPX. A.

S E C R E T.

Copy No: 8

58th Divisional Order No: 2.

-*-*-*-*-*-*-*-*-*-*-*-*-*-*-*-

5th February, 1917.

1. The Units enumerated will move to-morrow in accordance with March Table attached.

2. All billets will be clear by 12 noon to-morrow.

3. Completion of moves to be reported to Divl. H.Q.

4. Divl. H.Q. will close at FROHEN-LE-GRAND at noon and re-open at LUCHEUX at the same hour.

R.M. Barrington-Ward Capt.
for Lt.-Colonel,
General Staff, 58th (London) Division.

Issued to Signals at 2:35 p.

Copy No: 1 173rd Inf. Bde.
2 174th .. ..
3 C. R. A.
4 "Q"
5. A.D.M.S.
6 A.D.V.S.
7 A. P. M.
8 Signals
9 Divl. Train
10 S. S. O.
11 Divl. Gas Officer
12 Divl. Bombing Officer
13 Camp Commandant
14-15 War Diary
16 File

MARCH TABLE for TUESDAY, FEBRUARY, 6th.

(Reference Map LENS. Sheet 11. 1/100,000.)

Column.	Units.	Present Position.	Destination.	ROUTE.		Remarks.
	293rd Bde.R.F.A. and Medium T.M.Battery.	MEZEROLLES.	LUCHEUX	DOULLENS -- BOUT-DES-PRES -- LUCHEUX.		To march at 9.30 am.
	H.Q. and No.1.Section 58th Signal Coy.	FROHEN-LE-GRAND.	LUCHEUX.	-do-	-do-	1. Column A will march as a column under orders of O.C. 3rd Field Ambulance.
	Divl. H.Q.	-do-	-do-	-do-	-do-	
	H.Q. Divl. Train.	-do-	-do-	-do-	-do-	2. Column to march at 10 a.m. in the order shewn. Starting Point at road junction on main FROHEN--DOULLENS road E. of FROHEN.
A.	509 Coy A.S.C.	-do-	-do-	-do-	-do-	
	Mobile Vety.Section	-do-	-do-	-do-	-do-	
	Sanitary Section	-do-	-do-	-do-	-do-	
	Cable Section.	-do-	-do-	-do-	-do-	3. 3rd Field Ambulance to join in rear of column at MEZEROLLES.
	3rd Field Ambulance.	REMAISNIL	BREVILLERS	-do-	-do-	

Company Order No. 2 by Capt W.J. Mickelburgh Cmdg. In the Field. "B"

Exchange. LUCHEUX Exchange will remain open until further notice under L/Cpl. Rumsey W.E. assisted by Spns. Dyson F.W. and Bruton R.J. The following Offices can be obtained from the exchange
58th Division "Q" branch.
XVIII. Corps.
C. R.A. 58th Division.
D.A.D.O.S. —"—
S.S.O. —"—
175th. Inf. Bde.
174th. Inf. Bde.

Sounders. Morse lines will be disconnected at 10 am on 20/2/17 and instruments will be packed up for transport.

Cable Detachments. One Cable Det. each from J and K sections will be detailed to reel up line to AMMERA whence they will proceed direct to HENU reporting on arrival to Signal Office.

Signal Offices. The Divisional Office will open at HENU at 10 am. 2-2-17.
173rd Bde. Office will close at

II

IVERGNY at 10 am on 20th. and re-open on arrival at SOUASTRE. Messages for this Bde. will be dealt with by 138th Bde. Office at SOUASTRE.

175th Bde. Office will close at LE SOUICH not earlier than 10 am on 21-2-17 and re-open at POMMERA at 10 am. same day.

174th Bde. Office will close at POMMERA at 10 am. 21st. and re-open on arrival at BAILLEULMONT under orders issued separately to O.C. Bde. Section 174th Bde.

Arrangements for taking over POMMERA Office are to be made direct as early as possible by Os.C. Bde. Sections concerned.

Bde. Sections during these moves will carry with them Sounders, transformers, telephones etc. loaned them by 58th Divisl. Signal Co. R.E.

Issued to Sections at 7-30 pm. 19/2/17

(Sgd) W.F. Bat[illegible]
CAPT. R.E.T.F.
for O.C. 58th DIVISIONAL SIGNAL CO. R.E.

Company Order No. 1 by Capt W. G. Michelmore
Cmdg. In the Field.

Move. H.Q. and No. 1 Section will move 20-2-17 to HENU.

Parades. First parade will be at 6-30 am. Officers' Kits to be ready in billets at 7-0 am.
7-30 am Breakfast.
9-45 am. Company will parade in full marching order in column of route on road outside ? stables ready to move off under LIEUT. GILL. All ranks will carry the unexpired portion of the day's Ration in haversacks. Wheel driver of each vehicle is to be in possession of pass showing his destination.

Billets. Billets and stables must be left in a clean and sanitary condition. They will be inspected by 2/LT. J.G. BEAZLEY who will render the required certificate to the Town Major before leaving.

Lorries. Lorries are to be loaded with all heavy gear not

Confidential.

Vol 3

War Diary of

58th. Divisional Signal Coy. R. E.

From Feb. 27th. 1917 To March 26th. 1917.

(Volume I.)

Instructions regarding War Diaries and Intelligence Summaries are contained in F. S. Regs., Part II. and the Staff Manual respectively. Title Pages will be prepared in manuscript.

WAR DIARY
or
INTELLIGENCE SUMMARY
(Erase heading not required.)

Army Form C. 2118.

Place	Date	Hour	Summary of Events and Information	Remarks and references to Appendices
HENU.	27/2/17	7.30 am	Testing and tracing fault on Sounder line to 173rd Bde. which showed contact with Sounder line to 147th Bde. Contact found & cleared at 2.50 pm. on main Corps HH route. Corps wire twisted.	
"	"	11.45 am	received request from Sigs 138th Bde. for one mile D. tron to go out for Battn. attacking GOMMECOURT. Demand passed with request for urgent delivery to A.D.S. 18th Corps.	
"	"	4.35 pm	Sounder to BASSEUX through. Signals good. Divl. Office now working 8 sounders.	
"	"	5.15 pm	Visit from A.D.S. 18th Corps and conference as to state of cable market, and maintenance of communication in the event of a move forward. Ten miles D. tron promised. Request made to him for 6 additional Operators to help work sounder circuits.	
"	"	mdnt.	Messages dealt with during the day 561 despatched 516 outward, 384 inward, total 1461	[illegible signature]
"	28/2/17	3.30 am	Received wire from Sigs. 138th Bde. reporting successful attack & urgently requesting cable. Phoned Sigs. 18th Corps Heavy Artillery who had been ordered to supply same. Earliest possible delivery promised.	
"	"	9.30 am	175th Bde. Office closed at POMMERA and opened at LA CAUCHIE 2 pm. Telephonic communication only established, via LA CAUCHIE exchange.	

2449 Wt. W14957/M90 750,000 1/16 J.B.C. & A. Forms/C.2118/12.

Army Form C. 2118.

Instructions regarding War Diaries and Intelligence Summaries are contained in F. S. Regs., Part II. and the Staff Manual respectively. Title Pages will be prepared in manuscript.

WAR DIARY
or
INTELLIGENCE SUMMARY
(Erase heading not required.)

Place	Date	Hour	Summary of Events and Information	Remarks and references to Appendices
HENU	28/2/17	9'45am	Saw by Staff and received suggestion of move of DHQ. to BAVINCOURT. No time or further details available.	
"	"	9'0am	4 Operators reported from 18th Corps.	
"	"	"	Army	
"	"	10'15am	Phoned. O.C. Sigs 46th Divn. arranging details of sending instruments and personnel to take over Divsl. Office.	
"	"	11am	Received 7 miles D. twin cable from Sigs. 18 Corps H.A. and despatched 3 miles by motor to Sigs. 138th Bde. received 11'20am	
"		"	2 Operators report from 18th Corps.	
"	"	"	Corps Wireless Officer reports and is sent forward with trench wireless set to install same in GOMMECOURT	
"		11'30am	Visited by Staff again. Former information confirmed and probable hour of opening at new station given as 8am, March 1st.	
"	"	"	Advanced party detailed under Capt BATESON to proceed early afternoon to BAVINCOURT and open up Divsl. Signal Office with 10-line cordless exchange.	
"	"	3pm	Visited by D.D. Signals 3rd Army	
"	"	3'15pm	Advanced party leaves for BAVINCOURT	
"	"	6'30pm	Sigs. 175th Bde. arrive BRETONCOURT with personnel, to effect relief and take over lines.	

2449 Wt. W14957/M90 750,000 1/16 J.B.C. & A. Forms/C.2118/12.

Army Form C. 2118.

Instructions regarding War Diaries and Intelligence Summaries are contained in F. S. Regs., Part II. and the Staff Manual respectively. Title Pages will be prepared in manuscript.

WAR DIARY
or
INTELLIGENCE SUMMARY
(Erase heading not required.)

Place	Date	Hour	Summary of Events and Information	Remarks and references to Appendices
HENU	28/2/17	9'0 pm	Lorry with advance party and instruments arrives HENU. Change of instruments effected.	W. E. [illegible]
"	1/3/17	5'0 am	Divisional Optn. Order No 11 received.	
"	"	6'5 am	Lorry with instruments + operators leaves HENU for BAVINCOURT. D.H.Q. closes HENU 8. am. opening at BAVINCOURT same hour.	
"	"	8-0 am	Divsl. Office HENU handed over to 46th. Division. Company leaves by road for BAVINCOURT 9'25 am. arriving BAVINCOURT 12'55 pm.	
BAVINCOURT	"	8'0 am	Through to new H.Q. 173rd and 175th Bdes. by phone.	
.	.	9'0 am	" " " " 174th Bde. by phone.	
"	"	"	6 Operators returned to 18th Corps. and 2 reported in their place.	
		9'30 "	Telephone through to 18th Corps	
"	"	10'30 "	Sounder through to Corps. Delay due to instrument being shaken on journey and lines being wrongly labelled.	
"	"	11 am	All Sounders working. Delay due to non-working of double current set as above and consequent shortage of Sounders.	
		4 pm	Last lorry load arrives from HENU.	
"	2/3/17	9 am	Visited 173, 174 and 175 Bdes and respective Bde Signal Offices.	W. E. [illegible]
"	3/3/17	2'30 pm	All communications working OK.	
"	"	"	Visited Divsl. Supply Column re handing over Triumph Motor-cycles	W. E. [illegible]

Army Form C. 2118.

Instructions regarding War Diaries and Intelligence Summaries are contained in F. S. Regs., Part II. and the Staff Manual respectively. Title Pages will be prepared in manuscript.

WAR DIARY
or
INTELLIGENCE SUMMARY
(Erase heading not required.)

Place	Date	Hour	Summary of Events and Information	Remarks and references to Appendices
BAVINCOURT	4/3/17	9-30 am – 3'30 pm	Inspected Divisional Routes in the Area. Visited BEAUMETZ dugout and made arrangements for posting two linemen there.	
"	"	4'30 pm	Direct line and both Bde. laterals to 173 Bde. at BASSEUX broken by shell fire.	
"	"	5'10 "	Communication re-established	
"	"	10'45 "	58th Divl. Operation Order 12 received and acknowledged.	[illegible]
"	5/3/17	9-0 am	Arrangements made for communication with POMMIER, by Operation Order No. 3 issued to Bde. Sections by 12 noon D.R. [illegible]	Appx. A.
"	"	12'20 pm	C.R.E. Operation Order No. 8. received + acknowledged.	
"	"	2'15 pm	Received notification from General Staff that 200th and 231st Bdes R.F.A. would be under tactical orders of O.C. 58th Division.	
"	"	2'45 pm.	Visited 175 and 173 Bdes and arranged final details for communications on the Division taking over an extended front.	
"	"	4'10 pm	Received notification from General Staff of cancellation of Operation Order No. 12. pending further instructions. Company Operation Order No. 3 therefore cancelled.	
"	"	6'30 pm	Direct route to 173rd Bde BASSEUX broken by shell fire. Telephonic communication obtained via 174th Bde. Sounder line re-established 8'10 pm.	
"	"	8'5 pm	Received 58th Divn. Order No. G 401. + acknowledged.	
"	"	12 mdnt.	Received 58th Divn. Opn. Order No. 13 + acknowledged.	[illegible]

2449 Wt. W14957/M90 750,000 1/16 J.B.C. & A. Forms/C.2118/12.

Army Form C. 2118.

WAR DIARY
or
INTELLIGENCE SUMMARY
(Erase heading not required.)

Instructions regarding War Diaries and Intelligence Summaries are contained in F. S. Regs., Part II. and the Staff Manual respectively. Title Pages will be prepared in manuscript.

Place	Date	Hour	Summary of Events and Information	Remarks and references to Appendices
BAYINCOURT	6/3/17	9'5am	All lines working O.K.	
"	"	10 am	Inspected line to 173 Bde. which had been broken by shell fire, to consider whether same could be advantageously re-built in a different position. Decided to the contrary.	
"	"	"	No. 4. Section took over D. Sector from No. 2 Section. No. 3 Section took over Z2 Sector from 137 Bde. Coy. O.O. 4 issued.	Appx C.1.
"	"	4pm	Received intimation from General Staff that 173rd Bde. would, on the 7th. inst. take over Z.1. Sector from 137 Bde. Nessary arrangements for communication made accordingly.	
"	"	4'30pm	CRE's Operation Order No. 9 received & acknowledged.	
"	"	7'45pm	58th Divsl. Operation Order No. 14 received & acknowledged.	
"	"	"	Coy. Operation Order No. 5 issued. Copies attached.	Appx. B.
"	7/3/17	9'30am	Visited No. 3 Section and inspected communications in trenches. Visited 7th. Battn. BERLES & Advanced Telephone Exchange BERLES, and 5th Battn. in FARNBORO' RD. Communications to latter Battn. unsatisfactory and alternative means discussed with Bde. Section Officer.	A.G.[illegible]
"	"	"	No. 2 Section moves to POMMIER.	
"	"	1 pm	Arrived POMMIER, walking from BERLES. Saw communications were satisfactory, returning to HQ at 3'30 pm.	

2449 Wt. W14957/M90 750,000 1/16 J.B.C. & A. Forms/C.2118/12.

Army Form C. 2118.

WAR DIARY
or
INTELLIGENCE SUMMARY
(Erase heading not required.)

Instructions regarding War Diaries and Intelligence Summaries are contained in F. S. Regs., Part II. and the Staff Manual respectively. Title Pages will be prepared in manuscript.

Place	Date	Hour	Summary of Events and Information	Remarks and references to Appendices
BAVINCOURT	7/3/17	1'15pm	Divisional lines through and working to new Bde. Office by 1'15 pm.	
"	"	2'0pm	173rd Bde. Office opens at POMMIER	
"	"	4'0pm	Visited by A.D.S. 18th Corps and discussed communications from Division to Corps in the event of an advance. Decided existing communications unsatisfactory and that it is essential to build a main trunk airline route to BRETONCOURT. Points fixed; details of route to be decided later. Agreed that Corps should build H. comic route from BASSEUX to BRETONCOURT and Division from BASSEUX to BAILLEULMONT.	W. G. [illegible]
"	8/3/17	9'15am	Surveying route in company with Corps Signal Officer and details fixed. Work to commence 7'30 am. on the 9th. Returned 4'45 pm.	
"	"	7'45pm	Left with two lorries containing Signal stores; dumps made above BAILLEULVAL and BASSEUX returning 11-0 pm. Work in progress trying to clear up main bury LA CAUCHIE to POMMIER.	
"	9/3/17	7'30am	Parties despatched to BASSEUX to start on H. comic route; marking route etc.	W. G. [illegible]
"	"	3'30pm	Conference with Corps Area Signal Officer concerning buries in the Area.	
"	"	9'0pm	Received information from Signal Officer 173rd. Bde. that Signal Office had been heavily shelled and had retired to dugout.	
"	10/3/17	7'0am	Work on H. comic route continued	W. G. [illegible]
"	"	9'0am	Visited 173rd Bde. and decided that Signal Office would remain in dugout. Estimate made of cable required. Proceeded thence to inspect lines forward of Bde. H.Q. up to Batty. H.Q. returning 12'50 pm.	

2449 Wt. W14957/M90 750,000 1/16 J.B.C. & A. Forms/C.2118/12.

Instructions regarding War Diaries and Intelligence Summaries are contained in F. S. Regs., Part II. and the Staff Manual respectively. Title Pages will be prepared in manuscript.

WAR DIARY
or
INTELLIGENCE SUMMARY

(Erase heading not required.)

Army Form C. 2118.

Place	Date	Hour	Summary of Events and Information	Remarks and references to Appendices
BAVINCOURT	10/3/17	2'30pm	Left D.H.Q. to inspect comic route being built by Corps Signal Officer, and Divisional H comic route, returning 5'15 pm.	
"	"	6'30pm	Rung up by H.Q. R.A. and informed that 293rd were taking over from 231st. A.F.A. Bde. at POMMIER that same night. 293rd. Bde. without a single exchange.	
"	"	8'0pm	Three buzzer exchanges obtained and handed over to H.Q. R.A.	
"	"	9'30pm	'Phone conversation with A.D.S. 18th Corps. Reported that communication with Centre Batt. Centre Bde. unsatisfactory. See entry on 7th inst. above. Agreed to lay metallic D5. across the open. Rung up Sigs. 174th. and arranged to survey route with him on Sunday night 11th. inst. Line to be laid on Monday night 12th. inst.	
"	"	9'30pm	C.R.E's. Operation Order No. 10. received & acknowledged.	
"	11/3/17.	8'0am	Received H.Q. 58th Division memo. G.S. 267. dealing with probable advance of 46th. Division. Acknowledged.	R.G.K.
"	"	9'0am	Visited H.Q., R.A., and requested that in future earlier information of moves might be given to Sigs. R.A. Staff agreed. Arranged finally that Officer i/c Signals Divisional Artillery should live and mess with R.A. Staff.	
"	"	3'30pm	Rung up Sigs. 174th. Bde. and learnt that 5th Batt. was leaving FARNBOROUGH RD. for BERLES. Arrangements for laying metallic circuit cancelled and A.D.S. informed.	

2149 Wt. W14957/M90 750,000 1/16 J.B.C. & A. Forms/C.2118/12.

Instructions regarding War Diaries and Intelligence Summaries are contained in F. S. Regs., Part II. and the Staff Manual respectively. Title Pages will be prepared in manuscript.

WAR DIARY
or
INTELLIGENCE SUMMARY
(Erase heading not required.)

Army Form C. 2118.

Place	Date	Hour	Summary of Events and Information	Remarks and references to Appendices
BAVINCOURT	11/3/17	5'30pm	Inspected all Divisional lines leading out of BAVINCOURT.	
"	12/3/17	8'0am	58th. Division Instructions No. 1 Received and acknowledged.	[signature]
"	"	9'30am	Proceeded to 173rd. Bde. and discussed fully arrangements for communications during advance. Visited 1st. Battn. H.Q. BERLES. Selected central visual station at E.3 a. 8.0. Proceeded via Shell Street to front line and arranged runner posts from front to rear. also details of wire communications which would be necessary, returning 4'30 pm. Work:- Comic route lead in on D.5. cable to BRETONCOURT. Comic line built into POMMIER affording alternative telephone pair.	
"	13/3/17	9am.	Parties sent out to dismantle derelict lines and collect airline stores.	[signature]
"	"	10'30am.	58th Division warning order received.	
"	"	2'0pm	Visited 174th. Bde. and held conference with Bde. and Battn. Signal Officers. 5th. Battn. Signal dugout had been blown in. Four miles cable required urgently. Discussed communications in event of an advance. Returned 5'30pm.	
"	"	4'30pm	58th. Divsl. Operation Order No. 17 received and acknowledged.	
"	"	5'40pm	'Phoned A.D.A.S. XVIII Corps and obtained allotment of 4 miles D.twin. Advised Signals 174th. Bde. accordingly.	

2449 Wt. W14957/M90 750,000 1/16 J.B.C. & A. Forms/C.2118/12.

Army Form C. 2118.

Instructions regarding War Diaries and Intelligence Summaries are contained in F. S. Regs., Part II. and the Staff Manual respectively. Title Pages will be prepared in manuscript.

WAR DIARY
or
INTELLIGENCE SUMMARY
(Erase heading not required.)

Place	Date	Hour	Summary of Events and Information	Remarks and references to Appendices
BAVINCOURT	13/3/17	7'15pm	58th. Divsl. Operation Order No. 16 received and acknowledged.	
"	"	10'0am	2/LT. BEAZLEY and 3 Divsl. linemen attached to 173rd. Bde. ready for the advance.	
"	14/3/17	10 am	Received message G574 from G.S. 58th Div. cancelling ~~[illegible]~~ Artillery Bombardment mentioned in O.O. 16. of 13/3/17.	[illegible signature]
"	"	9am	58th Divl. O.O. No. 18 received & acknowledged.	
"	"	10 am	Visited 175th Inf. Bde. communications in trench area returning 4'30 pm.	
"	"	"	2/Lt. G.D. ARDEN surveyed route from V.6 b.4.5. to W.2a.3.3.	
"	15/3/17	9'30am	Visited communications up to Artillery Bdes. returning at 4.0pm.	[illegible signature]
"	16/3/17	9'30am	Inspected LA CAUCHIE test dugout and test boxes on the main LA CAUCHIE-POMMIER ~~[illegible]~~ bury. Arranged for second line to be put through to BERLES. Line surveyed on the 14th inst. marked ready for building. Straightening Cabs into Office.	
"	17/3/17	11'30am.	Visited by A.D. Signals 18th Corps. re proposed route to BAILLEULMONT. Building to depend on stores available.	[illegible signature]
"	18/3/17	8'0am	Party under Capt. Bateson build 2-way comic from BERLES to MONCHY preparatory to move of 173rd Bde. from POMMIER. Line complete, ringing and speaking good, by 3 pm.	
"	"	9'0am.	Visited 174th. Bde. and arranged for lines to be handed over in case of an advance and DHQ moving to BAILLEULMONT. Visited MONCHY and RANSART, returning 3 pm.	

2449 Wt. W14957/M90 750,000 1/16 J.B.C. & A. Forms/C.2118/12.

Army Form C. 2118.

WAR DIARY
or
INTELLIGENCE SUMMARY
(Erase heading not required.)

Instructions regarding War Diaries and Intelligence Summaries are contained in F. S. Regs., Part II. and the Staff Manual respectively. Title Pages will be prepared in manuscript.

Place	Date	Hour	Summary of Events and Information	Remarks and references to Appendices
BAVINCOURT	18/3/17	2.15pm	Received 58th Divsl. O.O. 19. and acknowledged.	
"	"	6.15pm	Lorry despatched to BRETENCOURT with all available airline stores, also forage and rations for airline detachment for one day.	
"	"	6.30pm	Received 58th Divsl. O.O. 20 and acknowledged.	
"	"	6.45pm	Airline detachment returning from BERLES diverted to BRETENCOURT	
"	"	11.30pm	30-cwt. lorry on return journey from BRETENCOURT sticks in the mud.	W.G.[illegible]
"	19/3/17	12.5am	C.R.E. Operation Order No 13. received & acknowledged.	
"	19/3/17	6am	Party from BRETENCOURT proceed to R32 a 6.5. to lay single D.twin line to RANSART	
"	"	7am	Remainder of linemen party under 2/LT. ARDEN commence building 4-way comic route from BRETENCOURT to FICHEUX.	
"	"	6.30am	Two miles D.twin sent Sigs. 175th Bde.	
"	"	6.45am	Divsl. Supply Column advised re 30-cwt. lorry and promised to send breakdown gang	
"	"	9.15am	2/LT. BEAZLEY with Infantry party leaves BERLES to dismantle 2-way comic route built previous day to MONCHY.	
"	"	9.20am	173rd Bde. Office, POMMIER closed down.	
"	"	10.15am	Party of two motor-cyclists 4 Operators and 4 cyclist orderlies sent forward to BRETENCOURT.	
			Contact during morning on Brigade Lines to 175th and 173rd. Unable to work sounder and telephone simultaneously.	
"	"	10.20am	Informed by General Staff on 'phone that 175th Bde. were moving to quarry South of BLAIREVILLE. No.4 Section running D. twin line to new position.	

2149 Wt. W14957/M90 750,000 1/16 J.B.C. & A. Forms/C.2118/12.

Instructions regarding War Diaries and Intelligence Summaries are contained in F. S. Regs., Part II. and the Staff Manual respectively. Title Pages will be prepared in manuscript.

WAR DIARY
or
INTELLIGENCE SUMMARY
(Erase heading not required.)

Army Form C. 2118.

Place	Date	Hour	Summary of Events and Information	Remarks and references to Appendices
BAVINCOURT	19-3-17	10'30am	Through to 2QC at RANSART on the phone.	
"	"	10'45am	Despatched 4 Operators, 2 Motor Cyclists and 4 push cyclists for opening report centre at BRETENCOURT	
"	"	11'15am	Informed by Sigs. 175th Bde. that Bde. HQ. would be at FICHEUX.	
"	"	12'45pm	Sounder working to 173rd Bde. RANSART.	
"	"	"	Building air-line BRETENCOURT to BLAIREVILLE. Poles erected ready for running wire at 6 pm.	
"	"	4pm.	Despatched rations to BRETENCOURT, also 2 miles D twin.	
"	"	6pm	58th Division transferred to VII. Corps. Line from VII Corps arrived 5'50 pm., placed on ringing phone exchange and working satisfactorily 6'3 pm. Sounder superimposed 6'5 pm. Signals good.	
"	"	8'30pm	Received telephone message from Sigs. 173rd Bde. that 173rd Bde HQ. are moving to BOIRY-ST-MARTIN early next morning. Phoned Gen. Staff for confirmation and issued orders accordingly.	
"	20/3/17	5am	Cable Det. with 8 miles D5. cable leaves BAVIN COURT for BRETENCOURT	[signature]
"	"	5am	Two miles D. twin sent from BRETENCOURT to 173rd Bde. at RANSART.	
"	"	6'15am	Cable wagon leaves BRETENCOURT with instructions to lay single line from BLAIREVILLE to BOIRY-ST-MARTIN. Airline party proceed, wiring route to BLAIREVILLE.	
"	"	7'45am	Proceeded to BRETONCOURT by lorry and wired in sounder for superimposing to 173rd Bde. which is moving from RANSART.	
"	"	"	Obtained from G.O.C. 175th Bde. use of troop of 18th Corps Cavalry to maintain communication. This arrangement confirmed by Gen. Staff 58th Division.	

2449 Wt. W14957/M90 750,000 1/16 J.B.C. & A. Forms/C.2118/12.

Army Form C. 2118.

WAR DIARY
or
INTELLIGENCE SUMMARY
(Erase heading not required.)

Instructions regarding War Diaries and Intelligence Summaries are contained in F. S. Regs., Part II. and the Staff Manual respectively. Title Pages will be prepared in manuscript.

Place	Date	Hour	Summary of Events and Information	Remarks and references to Appendices
BAVINCOURT	20/3/17.	(contd)	Following posts arranged :- BRETENCOURT 6 men; RANSART 6 men; HENDECOURT 4; BOIRY-ST-MARTIN 6. Troupe leaves BRETENCOURT for these posts at 10'30 am. Proceeded by road to BOIRY-ST-MARTIN via BLAIREVILLE and HENDECOURT. Cable wagon in BOIRY-ST-MARTIN at 11 am. Searched village throughout for H.Q. 173rd Bde, of which there was no trace.	
"	20/3/17	12'30pm	Found Signal Officer 173rd Bde. and arranged Bde H.Q. with him. Line established and working satisfactorily to BRETENCOURT 1 pm. Bde. Staff not arrived.	
"	"	2 pm	Left BOIRY-ST-MARTIN to visit mounted despatch posts. Outside HENDECOURT met troupe proceeding en masse to BOIRY-ST-MARTIN. Found same had been sent on by 173rd Bde. Despatched posts to their original locations. Posts re-established by 2'45 pm. Returned to BRETENCOURT 3'15 pm.	
"	"	7'15pm	Returned to BAVINCOURT.	
"	"	7'30pm	Received intimation that Divl. H.Q. would move to POMMIER at an early date. Obtained details from G 9'0 pm.	
"	"	9'5pm	Phoned O.C. Det. BRETENCOURT ordering cable wagon and working party to report to Capt. BATESON at BERLES 8'30 am next morning. Issued orders for lorry to leave BAVINCOURT for BRETENCOURT 5'30 am and take airline stores to BERLES	
"	"	9'20pm	Phone message from Gen. Staff. stating that move of D.H.Q. cancelled pro tem.	
"	"	9'30pm	Original arrangements allowed to stand full details of route worked out and working parties detailed	W.S.[illegible]

2449 Wt. W14957/M90 750,000 1/16 J.B.C. & A. Forms/C.2118/12.

Instructions regarding War Diaries and Intelligence Summaries are contained in F. S. Regs., Part II. and the Staff Manual respectively. Title Pages will be prepared in manuscript.

Army Form C. 2118.

WAR DIARY
or
INTELLIGENCE SUMMARY
(Erase heading not required.)

Place	Date	Hour	Summary of Events and Information	Remarks and references to Appendices
BAVINCOURT	21/3/17	10'15am	Metallic circuit from BRETENCOURT to BOIRY completed. Sounder superimposed, working direct from BAVINCOURT to BOIRY.	
		10'30am	Warning information from Gen. Staff that 174th & 175th Bdes. would be moving early on the 22nd. from their present stations. Probable destinations POMMIER and LA CAUCHIE. Arrangements made accordingly.	
		10'45am	58th Divn. O.O. 22 received + acknowledged	
		11'15am	Left BAVINCOURT for BERLES to inspect working party on airline route. Proceeded thence to BRETENCOURT, and thence by horse to BOIRY-ST-MARTIN. Bde. Staff interviewed, who report communications satisfactory. Returned to BAVINCOURT 6'15 pm.	
		4'15pm	Preliminary Orders issued to Mounted Troop, XVIII Corps at BRETENCOURT to move to BERLES and open mounted post there at 10am 22nd. Posts at BERLES, RANSART, HENDECOURT and BOIRY-ST-MARTIN.	
		7pm	Received intimation from Q Staff that 175th Bde. would probably move to BERLES and not LA CAUCHIE. Arrangements made accordingly.	
		10'45pm	O.O. No 6. issued.	Appx C2
		"	Orders issued to O.C. Mounted Troop.	Appx D.
"	22/3/17	9'15am	175th Bde. Office closed at BRETENCOURT.	W. G. [signature]
"	"	10'30am	174th. Bde. Office closed BAILLEULMONT and opened POMMIER	
"	"	2'0pm	Visited 175th Bde. Berles and thence inspected comic airline route built from BERLES to ADINFER.	
"	"	2'15"	~~[struck out]~~ 175th Bde. opened at BERLES.	
"	"	5'0pm	Received and acknowledged 58th Divl. O.O. 23.	
"	"	10'30"	Phoned VII. Corps and informed no airline stores available. Work on main ADINFER trunk route suspended.	W. G. [signature]

2449 Wt. W14957/M90 750,000 1/16 J.B.C. & A. Forms/C.2118/12.

Army Form C. 2118.

WAR DIARY
or
INTELLIGENCE SUMMARY
(Erase heading not required.)

Instructions regarding War Diaries and Intelligence Summaries are contained in F. S. Regs., Part II. and the Staff Manual respectively. Title Pages will be prepared in manuscript.

Place	Date	Hour	Summary of Events and Information	Remarks and references to Appendices
BAVINCOURT	23/3/17	8 am	Two Dets. have, dismantling disused comic routes and collecting stores.	
"	"	10'15 am	Left for BERLES and BOIRY-ST-MARTIN, to prospect for German airline routes and buries, and collection of airline stores, returning 5 pm.	
"	"	5'45 pm	Received warning information that 56th Division would be relieved in the line on 28th inst. by 21st Division.	
"	"	8'15 pm	Phone message from O.C. 21st Div. Signals, arranging appointment to come and inspect lines following day at 9'30 am.	[signature]
"	24/3/17	—	Work as follows :- (1) Airline party building from HAMEAU FARM to ADINFER VILLAGE (2) Party regulating German airline route from ADINFER VILLAGE to SUGAR FACTORY. (3) Party building airline from W 22 d. 9. 2. to W 22 a 1.1. (4). Collecting airline stores from neighbourhood of ST. AMAND	
"	"	10 am.	O.C. 21st Div Signals arrives. Diagrams explained and proceeded thence to inspect routes to POMMIER, BERLES, ADINFER and BOIRY, returning 3 pm.	
"	"	11 am	30th Division open at BRETENCOURT. Line G.C. 63. put through to GC 120 at request of VII Corps	
"	"	5 pm	Party of 1 Officer and 9 O.R. report from 21st Divisional Hqrs. to look over lines prior to taking over Area.	

2449 Wt. W14957/M90 750,000 1/16 J.B.C. & A. Forms/C.2118/12.

Instructions regarding War Diaries and Intelligence Summaries are contained in F. S. Regs., Part II. and the Staff Manual respectively. Title Pages will be prepared in manuscript.

WAR DIARY
or
INTELLIGENCE SUMMARY
(Erase heading not required.)

Army Form C. 2118.

Place	Date	Hour	Summary of Events and Information	Remarks and references to Appendices
BAVINCOURT	24/3/17	8 pm	Company O.O. 7. issued.	Appx E
	"	"	H.Q. 58th Div Artillery through on new airline route to 291st Bde. ~~in~~ ADINFER WOOD and 290th Bde. BOIRY-ST-MARTIN. Signals good.	
	"		Messages dealt with on 24/3/17. Telegrams 705. Registered packets 447.	[signature]
"	25/3/17	7 am	Working party under Capt. BATESON at THE RAVINE move forward to ADINFER.	
		8 am	Mounted relay posts ADINFER WOOD and BOIRY closed down. Run made by Motor cyclists through to BOIRY direct.	
		8'10 am	Received & acknowledged Div. O.O. 24.	
			Work 25/3/17:— Wiring second pair from HAMEAU FARM to ADINFER VILLAGE and thence on German airline to SUGAR FACTORY, thence by cable to Inf. Bde. H.Q. BOIRY.	
		9'15 am	Proceeded to ADINFER directing work on second line through to Inf. Bde. Selected Bivouac sites. Visited 174th. Bde. saw all lines and wireless working satisfactorily, returning to BAVINCOURT 4 pm.	
		9'20 am	175th Bde. closed sounder at BERLES.	
		10'30 am	Telephone working at HALLOY to 175th Bde. through XVIII. Corps	
		"	No. 3 Section relieves No. 2 Section at BOIRY with 174th. Bde. No. 2. Section proceeds to POMMIER. Through on phone 3'30 pm.	
		12'30 pm	J. cable Section reports for duty from VII. Corps.	
		4'30 "	Visited by A.D.S. VII. Corps. General system of forward communication discussed. Divisional scheme approved but informed that no stores of any description	/were

2449 Wt. W14957/M90 750,000 1/16 J.B.C. & A. Forms/C.2118/12.

Army Form C. 2118.

WAR DIARY
or
INTELLIGENCE SUMMARY
(Erase heading not required.)

Instructions regarding War Diaries and Intelligence Summaries are contained in F. S. Regs., Part II. and the Staff Manual respectively. Title Pages will be prepared in manuscript.

Place	Date	Hour	Summary of Events and Information	Remarks and references to Appendices
BAVINCOURT	25/3/17	contd	were available. Recommended that J. cable Section should proceed to ADINFER and collect all possible stores from recovered territory.	
"	"	5.15 pm	New direct line to Inf. Bde. BOIRY-ST-MARTIN completed. Fault on line preventing through communication being established.	
"	"	7.0 pm	Orders issued to J. Cable Section as per entry at 4-30 pm. above.	[signature]
"	"	12 pm	Messages dealt with — Telegrams 817, Registered packets 374.	
"	26/3/17	7am	Lineman attends to fault on line to BOIRY, which was located between BERLES and THE RAVINE.	
			Working party at ADINFER poling cable line from SUGAR FACTORY to BOIRY. Regulating and improving German airline route and collecting German airline stores.	
		9am	J. Cable Sec. leave BAVINCOURT for ~~[illegible]~~ ADINFER.	
		10am	Visited BERLES and inspected new airline route, thence from RAVINE. Arrangements made for new lead-in at KE 3 returning 1.15 pm. Met O.C. Signals 21st Div. and arranged full details of relief. Advance parties to be sent from each Coy. on ~~[illegible]~~. Informed that 21st Div. H.Q. would be at ADINFER WOOD and discussed action to be taken. Scheme settled, but decided that no further work could be done by this Unit as men had already been fully worked. Work accordingly handed over to Corps Section and Cable Sec. of 21st Divn.	

2449 Wt. W14957/M90 750,000 1/16 J.B.C. & A. Forms/C.2118/12.

Army Form C. 2118.

Instructions regarding War Diaries and Intelligence Summaries are contained in F. S. Regs., Part II. and the Staff Manual respectively. Title Pages will be prepared in manuscript.

WAR DIARY
or
INTELLIGENCE SUMMARY

(Erase heading not required.)

Place	Date	Hour	Summary of Events and Information	Remarks and references to Appendices
BAVINCOURT	26/3/17	7 p.m.	Orders issued recalling working party from ADINFER. Lime to report at BAVINCOURT at 4 p.m. on 27th inst.	

58th DIVISIONAL No. 27 MAR. 1917 SIGNAL COMPANY, R.E.

W. G. Michelmore
CAPT. R.E.T.F.
O.C. 58th DIVISIONAL SIGNAL CO. R.E.

2449 Wt. W14957/M90 750,000 1/16 J.B.C. & A. Forms/C.2118/12.

Army Form C. 2118.

WAR DIARY
or
INTELLIGENCE SUMMARY 58 D Signal Coy
(Erase heading not required.)

Vol 4

Instructions regarding War Diaries and Intelligence Summaries are contained in F. S. Regs., Part II. and the Staff Manual respectively. Title Pages will be prepared in manuscript.

Place	Date	Hour	Summary of Events and Information	Remarks and references to Appendices
BAVINCOURT	27/3/17	4 pm	Capt. BATESON and working party return from ADINFER.	
"	28/3/17	1 pm	Advance party, 2/Lt ARDEN and 14 O.R. leave for LUCHEUX.	
	"	4 pm	Coy. O.O. No. 8 issued	Appx A.
	29/3/17	9.30 am	H.Q. and No. 1 Section leave for LUCHEUX arriving 1.30 pm.	
	"	10 am	BAVINCOURT Office handed over to 21st Div. Signal Co. R.E. All lines working O.K.	
LUCHEUX	"	4 pm	O.C. Sigs 174th Inf. Bde. reports arrival at LUCHEUX.	[initials]
"	"	"	Communication with all 3 Bdes. by telephone only. One telephone pair superimposed to XIX Corps. Telephone pair to XVIII. Corps. Telephone pair superimposed to 51st. Bde.	
"	"	9.30 am	S K Cable Det. (LT. J.C. WARRINGTON) (15 O.R and 13 horses) attached to H.Q. 58th Divil. Artillery, (with Signals 21st Division).	
"	30/3/17	7.30 pm	58th Divn. O.O. 25 received & acknowledged.	[initials]
"	31/3/17	10 am	Billeting party proceed to FROHEN-LE-GRAND returning at 2.0 pm.	
"	"	12 noon	Company O.O. 9 issued.	Appx. B.
"	"	12.15 pm	58th Div. O.O. 26 received & acknowledged.	
"	"	3.30 pm	Advance party (2/Lt ARDEN and 16 O.R) leave for FROHEN-LE-GRAND.	
"	1/4/17	9.45 am	H.Q. & No. 1 Sec. leave for FROHEN-LE-GRAND	[initials]
"	"	12 noon	Signal Office closes and opens at FROHEN-LE-GRAND same hour.	

2449 Wt. W14957/M90 750,000 1/16 J.B.C. & A. Forms/C.2118/12.

Army Form C. 2118.

Instructions regarding War Diaries and Intelligence Summaries are contained in F. S. Regs., Part II. and the Staff Manual respectively. Title Pages will be prepared in manuscript.

WAR DIARY
or
INTELLIGENCE SUMMARY
(Erase heading not required.)

Place	Date	Hour	Summary of Events and Information	Remarks and references to Appendices
FROHEN-LE-GRAND	1/4/17	12 noon	Communication — Telephone pair superimposed to XIX. Corps. Telephone pair to DOULLENS. Working to Bdes. by D.R. only.	
"	"	3'30 pm	Column arrives at FROHEN-LE-GRAND.	
"	3/4/17	11 pm	Divil. O.O. 27 received & acknowledged.	[illegible]
"	4/4/17	11 am	Advance party, Capt. BATESON and 16 O.R. leave for BUS-LES-ARTOIS	Appx. C.
"	"	9 pm	Coy. O.O. 10 issued.	[illegible]
"	5/4/17.	9'30 am	H.Q. and No. 1 Sec. leave for BUS-LES-ARTOIS, dismounted party by bus, arriving 3 pm. Column by road arriving 6'30 pm.	
"	"	12 noon	Divl. Signal Office closed at FROHEN-LE-GRAND and opened at BUS-LES-ARTOIS.	
BUS-LES-ARTOIS	6/4/17.	—	Communications:— Telephone pair to 5th Corps. (thro' 8-0 am 5th). Sounder superimposed (10'15 am 5th). Telephone pair & sounder to 175th Bde. (11'35 am. 5th). Telephone pair & sounder to 174th Bde. (1'10 pm 5th).	[illegible]
"	"	7 pm	Divl. O.O. 28 received & acknowledged.	
"	"	5 pm	Through to 175th. Bde at BUS-LES-ARTOIS.	
"	7/4/17	12 noon	Sig. Office 174th Bde. closes. Bde. proceeded to CAMP, BIHUCOURT, not in direct communication at that point.	[illegible]
"	9/4/17.	8 am	Sig Office. 175th Bde. closes at BUS-LES-ARTOIS. Bde. proceeds to MIRAUMONT. Not in direct communication at that point.	[illegible]
"	10/4/17	7 pm	Through to 2/7th Battn. Ldn. Regt. at MAILLY-MALLET by 'phone.	

Army Form C. 2118.

WAR DIARY
or
INTELLIGENCE SUMMARY
(Erase heading not required.)

Instructions regarding War Diaries and Intelligence Summaries are contained in F. S. Regs., Part II. and the Staff Manual respectively. Title Pages will be prepared in manuscript.

Place	Date	Hour	Summary of Events and Information	Remarks and references to Appendices
BUS-LES-ARTOIS	12/4/17	11 am	Visited by D.D.S. Fifth Army	[initials]
"	13/4/17	12'30	175th Bde Signal Office closes at MIRAUMONT and re-opens at ACHIET-LE-PETIT.	
"	15/4/17	9 am	173rd. Bde. Office closes. Bde. moves to ACHIET-LE-GRAND. No direct communication to that point.	[initials]
"	16/4/17	11 am	Advance party under 2/Lt ARDEN leave for camp at BIHUCOURT.	
"	"	7'30 pm	Orders issued for move of Unit to BIHUCOURT on 17th.	[initials]
"	17/4/17	9-0 am	Column leaves for camp at BIHUCOURT by road. Rear party under 2/Lt BEAZLEY remains at BUS.	
BIHUCOURT	"	4-pm	Column arrives in camp at BIHUCOURT	
"	"	4 pm.	Divl Signal Office closes at BUS and re-opens at BIHUCOURT.	
"	"	4 pm	Through to 5th Corps by phone & sounder.	
"	"	5'30 "	" " 174th Bde. at BIHUCOURT by phone & sounder.	
"	"		No direct communication with 173rd & 175th Bdes., (Connection obtained thro 5th Corps.)	[initials]
"	18/4/17.	3 pm.	2/LT. T.E. PALMER reports from V. Corps as X Establishment Officer.	
"	"	9 pm	Rear party arrives from BUS.	[initials]
"	19/4/17	noon	Instns recd. from H.Q. 58th Divn. for LT. J.S.W. STONE to proceed to 8th Divl. Signals for duty.	
"	"	"	2/LT. S.J. BEAZLEY proceeds to 173rd. Bde. as O. i/c Signals.	[initials]
"	20/4/17	5 pm.	SK Cable Detachment rejoins Unit from H.Q. Divl. R.A.	
"	22/4/17	10'30 am	Lieut J.S.W. STONE leaves for 8th Divl. Signal Co. R.E.	[initials]
"	26/4/17	10' am	Visited Supply Column at LOUVENCOURT reference damaged motor cycles for repair and replacement.	[initials]

[signature] CAPT. R.E.T.F.
O.C. 58th DIVISIONAL SIGNAL CO. R.E.

2449 Wt. W14957/M90 750,000 1/16 J.B.C. & A. Forms/C.2118/12.

Instructions regarding War Diaries and Intelligence Summaries are contained in F. S. Regs., Part II. and the Staff Manual respectively. Title Pages will be prepared in manuscript.

WAR DIARY
or
INTELLIGENCE SUMMARY
(Erase heading not required.)

58 D Signals
Vol 5

Army Form C. 2118.

Place	Date	Hour	Summary of Events and Information	Remarks and references to Appendices
BIHUCOURT	28/4/17	7pm	Reinforcement of 18 O.R. arrived from V. CORPS. (Cablemen etc).	
"	1/5/17	2pm	Received instructions from HQ 58th Divn. to collect 10 L.D. remounts at AVELUY. Party detailed under Dr. Sgt. Choat to proceed to ACHIET-LE-GD by 7'45 pm. and entrain for AVELUY.	WEh
	2/5/17	3'30pm	Ten L.D. Remounts arrived.	
	1/5/17	3-0pm	2/LT. ARDEN returns from Power Buzzer Course at 5th Army Wireless Coy.	
	1/5/17	-"-	2/LT. PALMER T.E. proceeds on 10 days leave to U.K.	WEh
	4/5/17	1pm	HQ 175th Bde. Sig Office closed at ACHIET-LE-PETIT. No 4 Section moves to C29 a 5.2 for temporary attachment to 2nd. Australian Division, stopping at FAVREUIL for night of 4/5/17.	
	5/5/17	3pm	Through to 175th Bde. by phone via V Corps, 1st Anzac Corps and 2nd Anzac Divn.	WEh
	6/5/17	12pm	2/LT. G.D. ARDEN leaves for Wireless Course at GHQ CAMPAGNE-LES-HESDIN.	
	10/5/17	8am	Capt. J.C. WARRINGTON proceeds on 10 days leave to U.K.	
	12/5/17	3pm	2/LT. T.E. PALMER returns from leave.	
	12/5/17	12'10pm	Signal Office 173rd. Bde close. No. 2 Section proceeds to C5a 3.3. (57c) for attachment to VII. Division.	WEh
	13/5/17	6am	175th. Bde. Signals report arrival at FAVREUIL. Returning to ACHIET-LE-PETIT.	WEh
	13/5/17	4pm	175th Bde Signals report arrival at ACHIET-LE-GRAND.	WEh
	14/5/17	8am	Advance party under Capt. W.L. BATESON leave for MORY to prepare for taking over communications from 7th Division	WEh

2449 Wt. W14957/M90 750,000 1/16 J.B.C. & A. Forms/C.2118/12.

Army Form C. 2118.

Instructions regarding War Diaries and Intelligence Summaries are contained in F. S. Regs., Part II. and the Staff Manual respectively. Title Pages will be prepared in manuscript.

WAR DIARY
or
INTELLIGENCE SUMMARY

(Erase heading not required.)

Place	Date	Hour	Summary of Events and Information	Remarks and references to Appendices
BIHUCOURT	14/5/17	12'30am	Received message from HQ 173rd Inf: Bde. that Signal Office had been demolished by shell-fire.	
			Casualties 5 O.R. killed and 5 O.R. wounded.	
			Proceeded to that point immediately with 3 operators, 3 linemen, instruments and stationery.	
	"	5'50am	Communication re-established	
			Power-buzzer working O.K. all the time	[initials]
	15/5/17	noon	174th Bde. Signals leave Camp G12 c+d and proceed to L'HOMME MORT	[initials]

2449 Wt. W14957/M90 750,000 1/16 J.B.C. & A. Forms/C.2118/12.

Army Form C. 2118.

Instructions regarding War Diaries and Intelligence Summaries are contained in F. S. Regs., Part II. and the Staff Manual respectively. Title Pages will be prepared in manuscript.

WAR DIARY
or
INTELLIGENCE SUMMARY
(Erase heading not required.)

Place	Date	Hour	Summary of Events and Information	Remarks and references to Appendices
BIHUCOURT	14/5/17	7pm	Divl. O.O. 30 received and acknowledged	
	15/5/17	6pm.	Cable Sections proceed to MORY to join advance party.	W.G.L.
	16/5/17	9.30am	Remainder of H.Q. and No. 1 Sec. proceed to MORY arriving 11-30 am.	W.G.L.
			Rear party of 6 O.R. under Cpl. Pugh remain at BIHUCOURT to operate 10-line exchange + sounder line to V Corps.	
			Communications taken over from 7th Divn. as follows:-	
			To V Corps, phone with duplex sounder superimposed.	
			" 173rd. Inf. Bde. phone with sounder superimposed	
			" 174th Inf. Bde. " " " "	
			" 186th " " phone.	
			" 5th Aust. Divl. H.Q. phone with sounder superimposed.	
			" 62nd. Div. Artillery, phone	
			" V. Corps. H.A. "	
			" 2nd Aust. Divl. Arty, phone.	
			Telephone installation completed, consisting of one 30-line switchboard and one 10-line ditto (R.A. exchange).	
MORY	17/5/17	7am	4-pair arm run from D.V. to ECA poles; clearing old German route from ECB pole to ECOUST ready for re-wiring. Route surveyed for 8 pairs from B24 b2.7. to 5th Aust. Adv. H.Q. VAUX	W.G.L.
"	"	4pm	Route surveyed for running armoured twin from ECOUST to BULLECOURT.	
"	"	4.30pm	2/LT. ARDEN returns from GHQ Wireless Course.	W.G.L.

2449 Wt. W14957/M90 750,000 1/16 J.B.C. & A. Forms/C.2118/12.

Army Form C. 2118.

WAR DIARY
or
INTELLIGENCE SUMMARY
(Erase heading not required.)

Instructions regarding War Diaries and Intelligence Summaries are contained in F. S. Regs., Part II. and the Staff Manual respectively. Title Pages will be prepared in manuscript.

Place	Date	Hour	Summary of Events and Information	Remarks and references to Appendices
MORY	18/5/17	5'30am	Dismounted detachment working from 62 d 99 to point 31 BULLECOURT.	
"	"	8 am	Airline detachment working from ECA to ECB poles. Corps Airline Section build from ECB to VAULX VRAUCOURT	W.G.L.
"	20/5/17	3 pm	No. 2 Section relieved by No. 4 Section preparatory to 173rd Inf. Bde. being relieved by 175th. Bde. in the line. No. 2 Section proceeds to take over Camp at BIHUCOURT formerly occupied by No. 4 Section.	
"	20/5/17 21/5/17	10pm 3am	Parties working on BULLECOURT AVENUE communication trench delayed by shell-fire and trench incomplete. Work on permanent forward communications suspended. Communication with the front line still maintained by power buzzers and lines which hold for short intervals during day and night. No safe lines possible owing to lack of communication trenches and shortage of labour for burying cable.	W.G.L.
	22/5/17	7'30am	Party of 15 men laying armoured cable under duckboards, BULLECOURT AVENUE. 500 yards laid and work then stopped owing to incomplete trench.	W.G.L.
	"	9'30pm	175th. Inf. Bde. relieve 174th. Inf. Bde. on taking over whole of Divisional Sector. Change-over of lines timed to take place 9'30 pm.	
	"	9'15pm	Change-over delayed owing to S.O.S. call on the front.	W.G.L.

2449 Wt. W14957/M90 750,000 1/16 J.B.C. & A. Forms/C.2118/12.

Instructions regarding War Diaries and Intelligence Summaries are contained in F. S. Regs., Part II. and the Staff Manual respectively. Title Pages will be prepared in manuscript.

WAR DIARY
or
INTELLIGENCE SUMMARY
(Erase heading not required.)

Army Form C. 2118.

Place	Date	Hour	Summary of Events and Information	Remarks and references to Appendices
MORY	22/5/17	10.20 pm	Change over commenced.	
	"	10.30 pm	All lines working O.K. to new positions. 175th Bde. H.Q. ECOUST and not L'HOMME MORT.	
	23/5/17	2 pm	200 yds. more armoured cable laid in BULLECOURT AVENUE. Trench still incomplete.	
		3 pm	Capt. J.C. WARRINGTON reports on return from leave.	
	24/5/17	9 am	Armoured cable laid in BULLECOURT AVENUE down to Railway Embankment. Parties testing bury in front of Ecoust. 4 pairs found O.K.	
		11 pm	Battn. H.Q. move back from BULLECOURT to Railway Embankment. Line working satisfactorily in spite of two direct hits on the trench.	
		9 pm	175th Bde. H.Q. open at L'HOMME MORT with advance report centre ECOUST. Lines with one exception working O.K. from L'HOMME MORT 7.30 pm.	
	25/5/17	9 am	80 yds. armoured cable laid in BULLECOURT AVENUE. Work on trench slow. Parties clearing up cable in ECOUST and diverting Divisional lines into ECOUST	
	26/5/17	9 am	Establishing O.P. Exchange at ECOUST CHURCH and closing down that at Bde. Advanced Test Station. Parties on BULLECOURT AVENUE and routes in front of ECOUST as yesterday.	

2449 Wt. W14957/M90 750,000 1/16 J.B.C. & A. Forms/C.2118/12.

Army Form C. 2118.

WAR DIARY
or
INTELLIGENCE SUMMARY
(Erase heading not required.)

58 D Signal Coy
Vol 6

Instructions regarding War Diaries and Intelligence Summaries are contained in F. S. Regs., Part II. and the Staff Manual respectively. Title Pages will be prepared in manuscript.

Place	Date	Hour	Summary of Events and Information	Remarks and references to Appendices
MORY	29/5/17		58th Division takes over front of 62nd Division. 173rd Inf Bde relieve 187th Bde. HQ in the line.	KHL
"	"	2 am.	Transfer of Signals completed by No. 2 Section at 173rd Bde, HQ at L'HOMME MORT.	
"	30/5/17	3.0 am	174th Inf Bde. relieve 175th Bde in the line. No. 3 Section complete transfer of Signals at 3.50 am. Rear Bde. HQ L'HOMME MORT, Adv. ditto ECOUST.	KHL
"	2/6/17	.	2/Lt. F. G. Bryant leaves No 4 Sec on ten days leave to U.K.	KHL
"	2/6/17	-0am to 7-0pm	Parties clearing Area ECOUST CHURCH to head of bury and making same 8-pair pole cable route. Building airline 800 yds, from NZ pole to Kite Balloon. ERVILLERS Ammunition dump placed on phone to L'HOMME MORT Exchange.	KHL
"	3/6/17	4 pm	Main EV-HM route broken by enemy shell fire (13" H.V.) in Section MYB-SLJ.	KHL
"	"	6.15 pm	Lines repaired and temporarily working.	
"	3/6/17		No. 4 Section proceed to L'HOMME MORT and ECOUST to relieve No. 3 Section, on 175th Inf Bde. taking over from 174th Bde.	KHL
"	4/6/17	12.50 am	Relief of Signals completed by No 4 Section.	KHL
"	4/6/17		No. 3 Section proceed to camp at MORY (Divisional Reserve)	KHL
"	4/6/17	7am-7pm	Building 4-pair comic route to 310 and 312 R.F.A. Bdes. Route stopped at Railway line at B.23.d. Reconstruction and maintenance party on EV-HM route	KHL
"	6/6/17	9.10 pm	Divisional O.O. 40. received.	KHL

2449 Wt. W14957/M90 750,000 1/16 J.B.C. & A. Forms/C.2118/12.

Instructions regarding War Diaries and Intelligence Summaries are contained in F. S. Regs., Part II. and the Staff Manual respectively. Title Pages will be prepared in manuscript.

WAR DIARY
or
INTELLIGENCE SUMMARY

(Erase heading not required.)

Army Form C. 2118.

Place	Date	Hour	Summary of Events and Information	Remarks and references to Appendices
MORY	June 7th	9am to 7pm.	Party constructing route from Divl HQ to proposed Adv. HQ 173rd. Inf. Bde. Existing route utilised from D.HQ to SL pole;	
		4pm	2/Lt S.G. BEAZLEY returns from leave.	W.L.B.
	June 8th	9am - 7pm.	Work on line to proposed Adv HQ 173rd. Inf. Bde. as on 7th inst. Two-pair airline route constructed from SL pole to Bde. HQ.	W.L.B.
	9/6/17.	noon.	Capt W.L. BATESON proceeds on 10 days leave to U.K.	
		3pm.	Two Drivers, one GS. Wagon and four L.D. Horses (For R.F.A. Subsections) arrive from Rest Camp CONTAY.	W.L.B.
	10/6/17.	9am	Draft of six O.R. arrives from SIGNAL DEPOT, Advanced Base.	
		9am - 1pm	Transfer & checking of Stores for R.F.A. Subsections carried out.	
		3pm	No. 5 Subsection proceeds to 290th. Bde. RFA. No. 6 Subsection to 291st Bde R.F.A.	
		9am	4 Operators, 3 linemen, and 3 cyclists with 2/CPL. H.J. HACKER in charge, proceed to HQ 173rd Inf. Bde. for duty.	W.L.B.
	"	11.30pm	Addenda to 58th Divl. O.O. 40 received.	
	11/6/17	11pm	Operations ordered under 58th Divl. OO. 40 postponed.	W.L.B.
	13/6/17	8.30pm	Company Operation Order No. 11. issued	Apdx "A"
	"	9.45pm	58th Divl. O.O. 42 received.	
	"	2pm	Signal Officer from 20th. Inf. Bde. reports for taking over 175th Inf. Bde. Sector.	W.L.B.

2449 Wt. W14957/M90 750,000 1/16 J.B.C. & A. Forms/C.2118/12.

Army Form C. 2118.

Instructions regarding War Diaries and Intelligence Summaries are contained in F. S. Regs., Part II. and the Staff Manual respectively. Title Pages will be prepared in manuscript.

WAR DIARY
or
INTELLIGENCE SUMMARY
(Erase heading not required.)

Place	Date	Hour	Summary of Events and Information	Remarks and references to Appendices
MORY	14/6/17	8 am	Direct line from Division run to Railway Embankment at U26c 7.1.	[illegible]
	"	11 am	2/LT. F.G. BRYANT reports from leave.	
	"	12 noon	Adv. 173rd. Inf. Bde. Office wired up and working. All signals O.K. Communication from these H.Q. to advanced Report Centre established with visual, power-buzzer, telephone, and usual pigeons and runners.	
	"	2 pm	Advance party of Signal Section 20th Inf. Bde. arrives to take over; and Signal relief complete at 175th Bde. rear at 11'25 pm, at 175th Bde. Adv. 12'10 am 15/6/17.	
	15/6/17	2'50 am	ZERO HOUR for attack 173rd. Inf. Bde.	
	"	3'00 am	Contact Aeroplane station established at 58th. Divl. H.Q.	
	"	"	All Bde. and Division lines working O.K. Diagram of communications attached	Apdx "B".
	"	9-0 am	175th Bde. H.Q. moves to Rest Camp at B28 A 9.3.	
	"	"	174th. Bde. H.Q. " " " " L'ABBAYE, MORY	
	"	noon	Attack of 173rd Bde. successful. All lines working well. Fresh line run from Test point T.P. 1. to 2/2nd Batt.	
	"	9'30 pm	2/Lt. G.D. ARDEN proceeds with Power Buzzer to A.R.C. to instal same in newly captured HINDENBURG front line. Progress checked by hostile barrage and counter attack.	[illegible]

2449 Wt. W14957/M90 750,000 1/16 J.B.C. & A. Forms/C.2118/12.

Army Form C. 2118.

WAR DIARY
or
INTELLIGENCE SUMMARY
(Erase heading not required.)

Instructions regarding War Diaries and Intelligence Summaries are contained in F. S. Regs., Part II. and the Staff Manual respectively. Title Pages will be prepared in manuscript.

Place	Date	Hour	Summary of Events and Information	Remarks and references to Appendices
MORY	15/6/17	mdnt.	Total telegrams through Divsl. Sig. Office today 796.	
	"	"	Received copy of Warning Order from Gen. Staff, ordering 175th Bde. to attack HINDENBURG front and support lines NW of BULLECOURT on night 21-22nd.	[illegible]
"	16/6/17	5'30am	2/LT. ARDEN and party leave A.R.C. for front line	
	"	7am	Hand-generator power buzzer installed; difficulty with Base. Signals not received at T.P. 1.	
	"	4pm	2/LT. ARDEN returns to T.P. 1.	
	"	8'30pm	Company Order No. 12 issued	Appx "C."
	"	9-0pm	174th Inf. Bde. relieve 173rd. Bde	
	"	mdnt.	Total telegrams through Divsl Sig. Office today 623	[illegible]
	17/6/17	9'10am	Signal relief of 173rd Bde. by 174th Bde. complete.	
	"	"	A.R.C. closed down, power buzzer withdrawn and Battn. H.Q. returned to line on Railway. Signal Officer 174th Bde. reconnoitres HINDENBURG front line from the KNUCKLE to the HUMP inclusive.	
	"	8'30pm	Line run from CHALK QUARRY to advanced Company in HINDENBURG front line. Line through at 7-am 18/6/17 working satisfactorily with occasional breaks. Power buzzer still not working.	

Instructions regarding War Diaries and Intelligence Summaries are contained in F. S. Regs., Part II. and the Staff Manual respectively. Title Pages will be prepared in manuscript.

WAR DIARY
or
INTELLIGENCE SUMMARY
(Erase heading not required.)

Army Form C. 2118.

Place	Date	Hour	Summary of Events and Information	Remarks and references to Appendices
MORY	17/6/17	9pm	New power buzzer to replace hand-generator power buzzer sent to the KNUCKLE in HINDENBURG front line. Party caught in hostile barrage and counter attack and exchange of instruments not effected. Attempt made to improve power buzzer earths without success.	
	"	mdnt	Total telegrams through Div. Sig. Office today 601.	WKA
	18/6/17	4am	Sector to be attacked by 175th Bde. reconnoitred with Bde. Sig. Officer and all arrangements made for installation of power buzzers, wireless, running of lines etc. No buried routes possible owing to lack of labour.	
	"	8am	All lines heavily shelled and broken in left Bde. area.	
	"	8'30pm	Advance party of 1 Officer 25 O.R. from MORY to 175th Bde. Adv. HQ beyond ECOUST to prepare for the attack.	WKA
	19/6/17	10'30am	News received from Gen. Staff that operation of 175th Bde is cancelled. Advance party re-called, returning to camp 2-30 p.m.	
		3pm	174th Inf. Bde close Adv. HQ and return to L'HOMME MORT.	
	"	8pm	Divl. OO 44 received ordering relief of 58th Divn. by 7th Divn. at 10 am June 21/17.	WKA
	20/6/17	~~[illegible]~~ 7pm	Signal Office at 174th Bde. Adv. HQ closes.	WKA

2449 Wt. W14957/M90 750,000 1/16 J.B.C. & A. Forms/C.2118/12.

Instructions regarding War Diaries and Intelligence Summaries are contained in F. S. Regs., Part II. and the Staff Manual respectively. Title Pages will be prepared in manuscript.

WAR DIARY
or
INTELLIGENCE SUMMARY

(Erase heading not required.)

Army Form C. 2118.

Place	Date	Hour	Summary of Events and Information	Remarks and references to Appendices
MORY.	20/6/17	10 am	Signal Office for 173rd Inf. Bde. established at A18 sheet 57D. on arrival of No 2 Section at that point for encampment. (ABLAINZEVELLE).	[illegible]
"	22/6/17	8.0 pm	Signal Order No. 13 issued	APX. "D."
"	23/6/17	2 pm	Advance party proceeds to COURCELLES to take over Div. Signal Office etc. from 7th Divn.	[illegible] [illegible]
"	24/6/17	9-0am	H.Q. 174th Bde. proceed to camp at COURCELLES. Signal Office closed at L'ABBAYE MORY 9 am.	
"	"	"	H.Q. and No 1 Secs. proceed by road to COURCELLES, and take over camp etc. from Sigs. 7th Divn.	
COURCELLES	"	4.30 pm	H.Q. 175th Bde. Signal Office closes at MORY. No 4 Section proceeds to LOGEAST WOOD.	
			1 Offr. & 18 O.R. of No 2 Section arrive at H.Q. Camp COURCELLES.	[illegible]
"	25/6/17	11 am		
"	"	6 am	Cpl. Pugh and 3 O.R. proceed to H.Q. 173rd Inf. Bde. for Signal Office duty.	[illegible]
"	26/6/17	10 am	MAJ. W.G. MICHELMORE and 2/LT. G.D. ARDEN proceed on 10 days leave to U.K.	[illegible]
"	"	"	LT. D.C. HENRY proceeds on 10 days leave to U.K. from 174th Inf. Bde.	
"	27/6/17	8 am	S.J. Detachment under CPL. TREPPASS proceed to assist 7th Divn Sigs. in dismantling SLA route.	[illegible]
"	28/6/17	3 pm	6 O.R. from 4th Corps Wireless Co. report with instruments for duty with Unit on formation of Wireless Section.	[illegible]

2449 Wt. W14957/M90 750,000 1/16 J.B.C. & A. Forms/C.2118/12.

Army Form C. 2118.

Instructions regarding War Diaries and Intelligence Summaries are contained in F. S. Regs., Part II. and the Staff Manual respectively. Title Pages will be prepared in manuscript.

WAR DIARY
or
INTELLIGENCE SUMMARY
(Erase heading not required.)

Place	Date	Hour	Summary of Events and Information	Remarks and references to Appendices
COURCELLES	June 29	9 pm	3 OR. report from 4th Corps for Wireless Section.	WRJ

W. R. Jackson Capt [illegible]

O.C. 58th DIVISIONAL SIGNAL CO. R.E.

2449 Wt. W14957/M90 750,000 1/16 J.B.C. & A. Forms/C.2118/12.

58th DIVISIONAL SIGNAL Co. R.E.

APPX. A.

Operation Order No 8. Mar 28/17.

1). H.Q. 58th Divn. will close at BAVINCOURT tomorrow 29th inst. at 10 am. and reopen at LUCHEUX at same hour.

2). H.Q. and No 1 Sec. of Div. Sig. Co. will move from BAVINCOURT to LUCHEUX under Capt. W.L. BATESON. Starting point, R.A. H.Q.'s, which will be passed at 9'30 am. Route ARRAS RD – MONDICOURT – LUCHEUX. Company will parade in full marching order ready to move off at 9'15 am., steel helmets to be worn, haversack rations and feeds to be carried. Officer i/c will see that regulation distance of 200 yds. is kept between Units.

3) All billets must be left in a thoroughly clean and sanitary condition. 2/LT. S.G. BEAZLEY will be responsible for inspecting all billets after departure of Unit and will obtain clearing certificate from Town Major for same.

4) 174th. Inf. Bde. will move tomorrow from POMMIER to LUCHEUX.

5) Signal Officer 174th Inf. Bde. will report on receipt hereof time of closing POMMIER Signal Office and reopening at LUCHEUX. On arrival at LUCHEUX he will report in person at Divisl. Signal Office and obtain instructions as regards lines.

6) Acknowledge by 'phone.

Issued at 4-0 pm. to
Sigs 173, 174, 175 Inf Bdes
+ Sigs. 58th Div Arty.
Copies to C.S.O. 1.
" " War Diary 2.

[signature]
CAPT. R.E.
O.C. 58th DIVISIONAL SIGNAL CO. R.E.

68th DIVISIONAL
SIGNAL Co. R.E.

APPX. "B"

Operation Order No 9. Mar. 31/17.

1). Divisional H.Q. will close at LUCHEUX 12 noon April 1st. and open at BOUQUEMAISON at the same hour.

2). The following moves of Bde. H.Q. will take place on the 1st. inst:— 173rd Bde. from POMMERA to BONNIÈRES; 174th Bde. LUCHEUX to VACQUERIE-LE-BOUCQ; 175th. HALLOY to NEUVILLETTE.

3). Communication during the move and after arrival at the new station will be by despatch rider only.

4). The attention of Officers i/c Bde. Signals is directed to War Divisional Standing Orders Sec. 3. para. 17 (g) which must be complied with as soon as ever Bde. H.Q. are settled down. In the event of the distance between Bde. and Divl. H.Q. being considerable a motor-cyclist may be used for this purpose.

5. Acknowledge.

Issued to Sigs. 174, 175 and 173rd. Bdes and Sigs 58th Div. Artillery by 12 noon. D.R.L.S.

[signature]
Capt. R.E.T.F.
O.C. 58th DIVISIONAL SIGNAL Co. R.E.

W.D.

APPX "C".

Orders by Capt. W. G. Michelmore Cmdg.
58th Divsl Signal Coy R.E. In the Field Apl 4/17

Operation Order No. 10.

1). Divsl. H.Q. close at FROHEN-LE-GRAND at 12 noon on 5th inst. and reopen at BUS-LES-ARTOIS at the same hour.

2) H.Q and No 1. Sec. will move by road to BUS-LES-ARTOIS under 2/LT. G.D. ARDEN. Starting point the Church FROHEN-LE-GRAND, which will be passed at 9'30 am by the head of the column. Route DOULLENS-SARTON-LOUVENCOURT. Reveillé will be at 5'30 am.

3). Halts will be made as under:- On main DOULLENS Road after passing HEM, one hour. At SARTON, one hour. At both halts all horses will be watered and fed.

4) Rations. 2/Cpl. Wood is placed in charge of rations and forage for Friday, which he will draw from the ASC at FROHEN Church at 9 am, superintend loading same on D.H.Q Motor Bus, travel with same to BUS and deliver same to C.Q.M.S.

5). Bus accommodation has been provided for 14 men, who will parade under C.Q.M.S. in full marching order at billet 44 at 9'30 am and await orders for embarking.

6) C.Q.M.S. will see that five 2-cwt. drums of cable are loaded on ASC ration

6 (contd).
wagon as soon as rations have been transferred therefrom as mentioned in para. 4. above.

7) Sergt. RIDGE and three O.R. will be left as rear-party to close Signal Office at 12 noon and journey to BUS-LES-ARTOIS. They will be provided with rations and forage up to midnight FRIDAY and will billet for the night at or near AUTHIEULE. They will not attempt to reach BUS that same night.

8)
No transport is to enter DOULLENS before 1 pm.

Issued to Sigs.
173rd. 174th. 175th. Bde.
9pm.
Copies to 2/LT. ARDEN, CSM
+ War Diary (2).

W. G. Michelmore
O.C.
58th. Divl Signal Co. R.E.

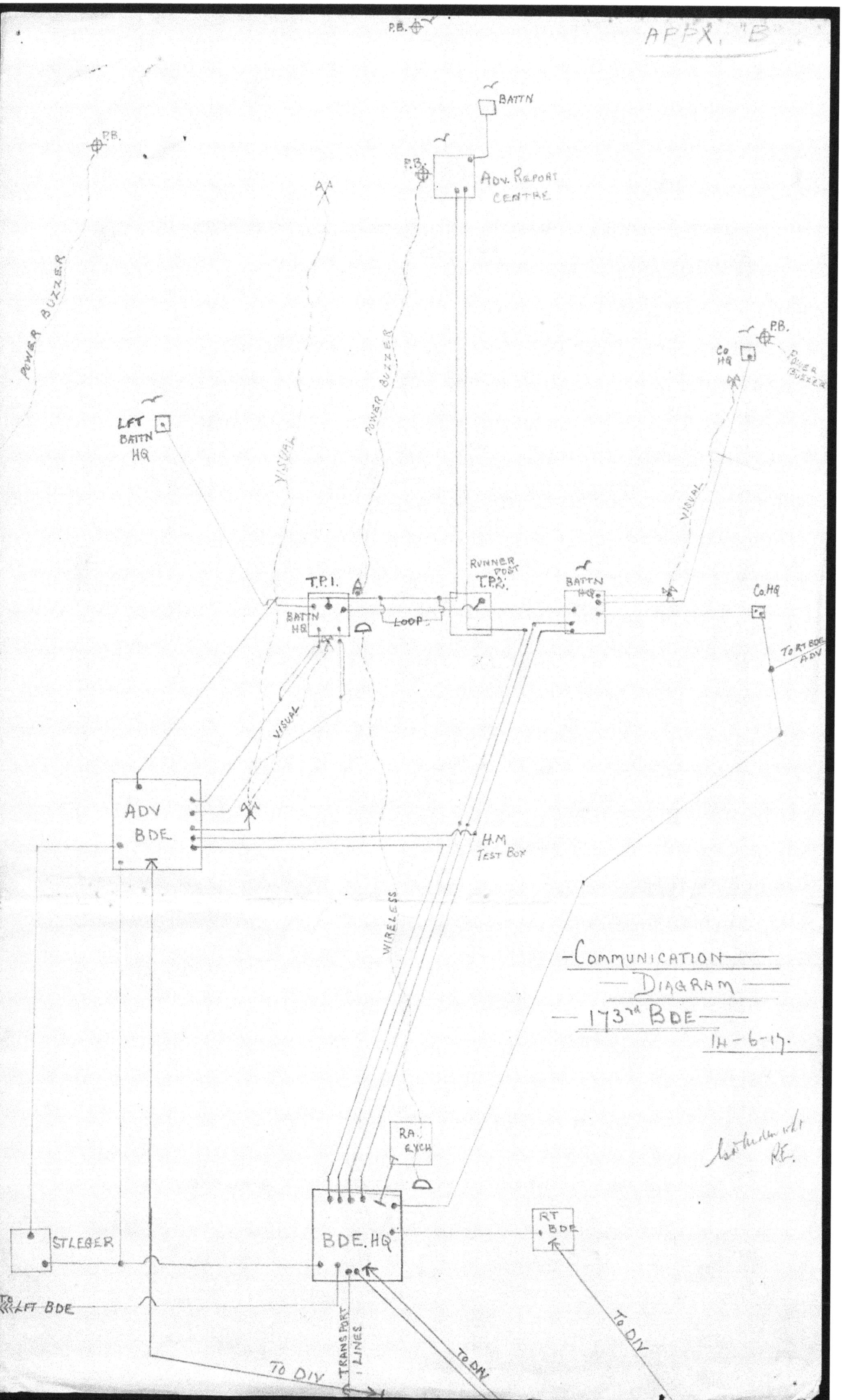

APPX. "B"

P.B.

BATTN

P.B.

ADV. REPORT CENTRE

P.B.

POWER BUZZER

VISUAL

POWER BUZZER

P.B.

Co HQ

POWER BUZZER

LFT BATTN HQ

VISUAL

RUNNER POST

T.P.1.

T.P.2.

BATTN HQ

BATTN HQ

LOOP

Co.HQ

TO RT BDE ADV

VISUAL

ADV BDE

H.M TEST BOX

WIRELESS

-COMMUNICATION-

DIAGRAM

173rd BDE

14-6-17.

RA. EXCH

RE.

STLEGER

BDE. HQ

RT BDE

TO LFT BDE

TRANSPORT LINES

TO DIV

TO DIV

TO DIV

58th DIVISIONAL SIGNAL Co. R.E. APPX "O"

Order No 12. June 16/17.

1). The 174th Inf. Bde will relieve 173rd Inf Bde [illegible] in the left sector of the Div. front, the relief of H.Q. to be complete at 9 pm and of troops at 3 am. on the 17th.

2). The following personnel [illegible] [illegible] after the relief is complete.

3 [illegible] at L'HOMME MORT.

2 [illegible] [illegible] — " —

1 " [illegible] — " —

2 " [illegible] at [illegible]

2 " " T.R.1.

Remainder of Signal personnel [illegible] at 173rd Bde [illegible] mentioned in para [illegible] above will remain with Signal Section 174th Bde until further orders. [illegible] 6" will [illegible] [illegible] [illegible] H.Q. as at present. All other Signal personnel in the sector will be left by Sig. 173rd Bde. [illegible] [illegible] [illegible] after which [illegible] will be rationed by Sigs. 174th Bde.

3) The following instruments will be handed over by 174th Bde [illegible] [illegible] similar instruments in use at [illegible] H.Q. —

4 panels 12-line 1 panel [illegible].

3

1 signal transformer & Buzzer Unit.
The above will be handed over in charge of
Signal Master L'HOMME MORT.
In addition to the above the following
will also be left at L'ABBAYE, MORY
in position ready for 173rd Bde.
to be taken over, in exchange for
instruments in similar positions
at [illegible] [illegible] [illegible] 174th Bde.
1 ten-line [illegible] exchange
2 [illegible] [illegible] [illegible].
4) Technical stores belonging to 173 Bde
Signal Section at [illegible] [illegible]
will be handed over to [illegible] [illegible]
at 174th Bde.
5) Signal Officers concerned will
arrange mutually for the relief of
all other exchanges, telephones etc.
in the Bde. sector.
The relief of the [illegible] [illegible]
[illegible] [illegible] [illegible] [illegible]
[illegible] [illegible] [illegible] [illegible]
Wireless and [illegible] [illegible] personnel
will remain [illegible] by
Officer 173rd Bde. [illegible] [illegible]
Sig. Officer 174th Bde. until 12 noon
on the 17th [illegible] [illegible] [illegible]
the situation demands [illegible] [illegible]
[illegible] [illegible] [illegible] [illegible] 24 hours.

after the remainder of the signal staff is complete :—

Signal [illegible] at L'HOMME MORT
2 linesmen at T.P. 1.
2 " at [illegible] Bde. HQ.

6). Signal relief will, if the tactical situation permit, be completed by 9 am June 17th. completion being wired to SIGS 58TH DIVN. the code word "BOB" being used.

7) Acknowledge.

(Sgd) [illegible] Major RE

8-30 pm

Issued to O.C. Signals 173rd Inf Bde
" 174th "
Copies to " 175th "
" [illegible]
" [illegible] Div RA
" File
" War Diary (2)

APPX. D. Copy 4

58th. Divisional Signal Co. R.E.

Signal Order No. 13.

22/6/17

Reference Sheet 57c NW. (1/20,000)

Move. (1). No. 2 Section of the Divisional Signal Coy. R.E. at present attached 173rd. Bde. will move from ABLAINZEVILLE to COURCELLES (U.15 c 1.2.) on the 25th. inst. reporting on arrival to O.C. 58th. Divisional Signal Coy. R.E. not later than 12 noon.

Personnel. 2.

(a). The following personnel of the Section will remain with H.Q. 173rd. Bde:-

Spr. Hoyal Spr. Rogers Cpl. Bastin
Pnr. Hogan Spr. Snowden.

(b) The following personnel of H.Q. Divsl. Signal Co. will report to H.Q. 173rd. Inf. Bde. by 9 a.m. on the 25th. Inst. and remain until further orders:-

Corpl. Pugh Spr. McMorran
Spr. Lakeman Spr. Tarring.

(c). Battn. runners, (not exceeding 4 per Battn.) will remain with the Signal details for purposes of intercommunication.

(d). All other Infantry personnel attached will return to their Batns.

Rations. 3. The Section will come rationed up till midnight 26th. inst. after which hour they will be rationed by H.Q. Divisional Signal Coy.

4. Please acknowledge.

Copy 1. Sigs. 173rd. Inf. Bde.
2. O. I/C H.Q., Divisional Signal Coy.
3. H.Q. 173rd. Inf. Bde. (for information).
4 and 5. War Diary
6. File.

[signature]
Major RE.
O.C. 58th Div. Signal Co RE

Army Form C. 2118.

58 D Signal Coy

Vol 7

WAR DIARY
or
INTELLIGENCE SUMMARY
(Erase heading not required.)

Instructions regarding War Diaries and Intelligence Summaries are contained in F. S. Regs., Part II. and the Staff Manual respectively. Title Pages will be prepared in manuscript.

Place	Date	Hour	Summary of Events and Information	Remarks and references to Appendices
COURCELLES	1/7/17	9am	Information received from G Staff reference relief of 42nd. Division and 59th Division by 58th. Division	W.R.J.
"	"	12noon	Visited Signals 42nd. Division at YTRES reference taking over.	W.R.J.
"	2/7/17	10am	Visited Signals 59th. Division at EQUANCOURT reference taking over	W.R.J.
"	2/7/17	8pm	58th Div O.O. 45. received and acknowledged.	W.R.J.
"	7/7/17	8am	advance party under 2/LT. PALMER leave for YTRES	W.R.J.
"	8/7/17	11am	Major W.G. MICHELMORE. and 2/LT. G.D. ARDEN return from leave.	W.R.J.
"	"	"	LT. D.C. HENRY returns to 174th Inf. Bde. from leave.	Appx A.
"	"	8pm	Company Order No. 14 issued	W.R.J.
"	9/7/17	6am	HQ and No. 1 move from COURCELLES to YTRES.	
"	"	10am	Signal Office closed at DHQ COURCELLES and re-opened at YTRES.	
"	"	"	Through to 175th Inf Bde. at Q 14 central.	
"	10/7/17	10am	Through to 173rd Inf Bde at NEUVILLE	[illegible]
"	"	11.20am	Through to 174th Inf Bde. at DESSART WOOD (W.1.b.2.5.)	[illegible]

WAR DIARY
or
INTELLIGENCE SUMMARY

(Erase heading not required.)

Army Form C. 2118.

Instructions regarding War Diaries and Intelligence Summaries are contained in F. S. Regs., Part II. and the Staff Manual respectively. Title Pages will be prepared in manuscript.

Place	Date	Hour	Summary of Events and Information	Remarks and references to Appendices
YTRES	11/7/17	10am	Warned that D. H.Q. would move in or about a weeks time from YTRES to EQUANCOURT	
"	"	11.30am	H.Q. 174th Bde. report moving from DESSART WOOD to HAVRINCOURT WOOD on following day.	
"	"	4.30pm	Move of 174th Bde. cancelled.	
"	12/7/17		58th Divl O.O. 46. received, ordering 173rd Inf. Bde. to relieve 174th Inf. Bde. and 174th Bde. to relieve 175th Bde. in succession	[signature]
"	13/7/17	7am	Route from METZ to S.E. corner HAVRINCOURT WD. commenced.	
"	"	2.30pm	174th Inf. Bde. move from DESSART WOOD to HAVRINCOURT WOOD (Q 15 C).	
"	"	7.45pm	58th Divl. O.O. 47 received cancelling O.O. 46. of previous day. Divl. front to be held by 3 Inf. Bdes. with 3 Battns. as Divl. Reserve	
"	14/7/17	noon	Route HW-HE broken in three places by shrapnel.	[signature]
"	"	10pm	H.W.-H.E. route again broken by shrapnel.	
"	15/7/17	7am–5pm.	METZ route to HAVRINCOURT WOOD completed; completing airline pairs to new 173rd Bde. H.Q.	[signature]
"	"	noon	Warning Order received from 58th. Division re relief by 9th Divn. on or about 25th inst.	[signature]

2449 Wt. W14957/M90 750,000 1/16 J.B.C. & A. Forms/C.2118/12.

Instructions regarding War Diaries and Intelligence Summaries are contained in F. S. Regs., Part II. and the Staff Manual respectively. Title Pages will be prepared in manuscript.

WAR DIARY
or
INTELLIGENCE SUMMARY
(Erase heading not required.)

Army Form C. 2118.

Place	Date	Hour	Summary of Events and Information	Remarks and references to Appendices
YTRES	16/7/17	8am.–4pm.	Airline pairs to 173rd Bde HQ completed.	
			HQ 173rd Bde move to Q34 a 28.	
		6pm	Through to new Bde HQ. 173rd. on 2 pairs. Sounder superimposed. Lines working satisfactorily.	[illegible]
	17/7/17	8am	HW-HE and HM routes completely broken down by shell fire. 174th & 175th Inf Bdes and 210 Bde R.F.A. cut off except for one faulty line (speaking only).	
	"	10.40am	Lines again working satisfactorily.	
	"	7am–7pm.	Party putting through new line to I.H. from RUYAULCOURT. Fresh tees for RE Dump, A.R.P, and Field Dressing Stn. off Corps airline route.	
	"	"	New lead-out from LITTLE WOOD, 8-pair airline, commenced.	
	"	"	Lateral line laid from I.H. to F.D.	[illegible]
	18/7/17	7am–7pm.	Strong reeling-up parties clearing up RUYAULCOURT. Lateral line laid from	
		"	FD to J.DA. Cables from JDA to NEUVILLE reeled up.	
		"	Airline lead-out completed.	[illegible]
	19/7/17	noon	Part-completed bury scheme in Divisional Sector inspected by A.D.S. IV Corps.	
	"	11.30pm	HM route again broken by shell-fire	
	20/7/17	7am	Two pairs obtained from Corps and put through to METZ via EQUANCOURT and FINS.	[illegible]

2449 Wt. W14957/M90 750,000 1/16 J.B.C. & A. Forms/C.2118/12.

Army Form C. 2118.

Instructions regarding War Diaries and Intelligence Summaries are contained in F. S. Regs., Part II. and the Staff Manual respectively. Title Pages will be prepared in manuscript.

WAR DIARY
or
INTELLIGENCE SUMMARY
(Erase heading not required.)

Place	Date	Hour	Summary of Events and Information	Remarks and references to Appendices
YTRES	20/7/17	11am	O.C. Signals 9th Division arrives to make preliminary arrangements for relief. Details of move etc. discussed.	
"		mdnt	Messages dealt with by Divl. Signal Office during the day. Telegrams 715, Despatches 455, Total 1170.	[signature]
	21/7/17	9'30pm	58th Divn. O.O. 48 received.	
	23/7/17	12'30pm	Administrative instructions in connection with 58th Divn. O.O. 48 received.	
	–"–	"	A.D.A.L.S. Order No 25 received	
	–"–	2pm	Advance parties of Signal Sections 26th and S. African Brigades of 9th Division arrive to take over from 175th and 174th Inf. Bdes. of 58th Division.	
	–"–	4pm	Signal Order No 15 issued	[signature] Appx "B"

2449 Wt. W14957/M90 750,000 1/16 J.B.C. & A. Forms/C.2118/12.

Army Form C. 2118.

Instructions regarding War Diaries and Intelligence Summaries are contained in F. S. Regs., Part II. and the Staff Manual respectively. Title Pages will be prepared in manuscript.

WAR DIARY
or
INTELLIGENCE SUMMARY
(Erase heading not required.)

Place	Date	Hour	Summary of Events and Information	Remarks and references to Appendices
YTRES	24/7/17	10.30am	C.R.E's Order No. 25 received.	
	"	mdnt.	Total messages for the day – Telegrams 703, despatches 599, total 1302.	
	25/7/17	noon	26th Inf Bde arrive at NEUVILLE BOURJONVAL	
	"	8pm.	58th Divn. O.O. 50 received, cancelling O.O. 49.	
	"	"	Signal Officer S African Inf. Bde arrives to take over from 174 Bde and is attached thereto.	[initials]
"	27/7/17	8am	175th Inf. Bde. H.Q. hand over command of left sector of Divl. Area to 26th Inf. Bde. Telephonic communication established to BERTINCOURT to pick up Battns. in "Staging Area".	
	"		Officer i/c Signals 27th Inf. Bde. arrives with advance party to inspect sector of 173rd Inf. Bde. to which formation he is attached.	
	"		Amendment to 58th Divl. O.O. No. 50 received.	[initials]
"	28/7/17	noon	1 Officer and Cable Section 9th Division report as advance party.	
"	29/7/17	8am.	Signal relief of 174th Bde by S.A. Inf. Bde complete.	
"	29/7/17	"	Wireless Section 9th Division report.	
"	"	7.30pm	58th Divl. R.A. Operation Order No. 15 received.	
"	"	8pm	Wireless at left Bde. H.Q. relieved.	[initials]
"	30/7/17	8am.	Advance party leaves for FOSSEUX under 2/Lt. G.D. ARDEN with Office relief.	

2449 Wt. W14957/M90 750,000 1/16 J.B.C. & A. Forms/C.2118/12.

Instructions regarding War Diaries and Intelligence Summaries are contained in F. S. Regs., Part II. and the Staff Manual respectively. Title Pages will be prepared in manuscript.

Army Form C. 2118.

WAR DIARY
or
INTELLIGENCE SUMMARY
(Erase heading not required.)

Place	Date	Hour	Summary of Events and Information	Remarks and references to Appendices
YTRES	31/7/17	6'15am	Party of 22 OR under 2 Lt. M.S. report to O.C. 249 Employment Co., proceed to BAPAUME by bus, thence to SAULTY by train, thence by road to FOSSEUX, arriving 10 pm. 31/7/17.	
"	"	9 am	Remainder of H.Q. & No 1. Sections leave YTRES with transport, and proceed to FOSSEUX by road, resting overnight at ABLAINZEVILLE.	
"	"	11 am	Signal Office YTRES handed over to 9th Div Sig Co. Sig. Office opens at FOSSEUX.	W.G.h
FOSSEUX	1/8/17	noon	Remainder of H.Q. & No 1 Sections, with transport arrive at FOSSEUX.	
"	"	2'30pm	58th Div. O.O. 51 received.	W.G.h

W. G. Michelmore
Major R.E.
O.C. 58th DIVISIONAL SIGNAL CO. R.E.

2449 Wt. W14957/M90 750,000 1/16 J.B.C. & A. Forms/C.2118/12.

58th DIVISIONAL SIGNAL Co. R.E.

Appx "B"

No. 6

Signal Order No. 15.

23-7-17.

1). (a) The 58th Division (less Artillery) will be relieved in the line by the 9th Division (less Artillery) between 26th - 31st July 1917.

(b) Inf. Bdes will be relieved as follows:-

175 Bde.	by	26th Inf. Bde.	on July 26th	& night	26/27 July
174	"	" 1st. S. African	" "	" 28th	" " 28/29 "
173	"	" 27th Inf.	" "	" 30th	" " 30/31 "

The command of each Sector will pass to Brig-Gen. Cmdg. relieving Bde at 8 am. on morning after completion of relief.

(c) Each Bde. on completion of relief will return to Staging area (BERTINCOURT, RUYAULCOURT and NEUVILLE BOURJONVAL) with Bde. H.Q. at the latter place.

(d). On relief the Division will concentrate in FOSSEUX area, with H.Q. as follows:-

Divl. H.Q.	FOSSEUX
173 Bde.	MANIN
174 "	BERNEVILLE
175 "	WARLUS

(e) Divl. H.Q. close YTRES at 11-0 am on 31st July reopening at FOSSEUX same hour.

2) Relief of Bde. Signal Sections will be carried out under arrangements made between Signal Officers concerned. Complete up-to-date circuit and route diagrams will be handed over in each case, duplicates being forwarded to these H.Q.

3). Each Bde. Section will leave the following stores wired in position and will be issued with an equal number on arrival in the rear area.

	Test panels 12-line	Test panels galvs.	Test panels 2-transformer
173 Bde.	2	1	1
174 Bde.	4	1	1
175 Bde	3	1	1

All other technical stores, including pigeon equipment, will be taken away, unless exchanged for a similar amount to the mutual satisfaction of Bde. Signal Officers concerned. Cable surplus to establishment will be handed over to relieving Bdes.

4. Relief of power buzzer and wireless equipment will be arranged by Officer i/c Wireless, 58th Division.

5) Commencing 28th July a D.R.L.S. will run from YTRES to FOSSEUX as under, and despatches for the ABLAINZEVILLE camp will be accepted by this run.

YTRES	dep	9'00 am
ABLAINZEVILLE	arr.	9'55 am.
-"-	dep.	10'00 am
FOSSEUX	arr.	11'10 am
"	dep	11'40 am
YTRES	arr.	1'40 pm.

Bdes. will make use of this D.R.[illegible] as far as possible in preference to "Specials".

6). Bde. H.Q. in NEUVILLE and BATTN. H.Q. in RUYAULCOURT are both connected to the Divl. Ringing exchange, and Bdes. will on arrival at NEUVILLE immediately get into touch with the Divl. Office, superimposing sounder only if desired to do so by Signalmaster YEH

7). On arrival in the FOSSEUX area Bde. Signal Officers will arrange with O.C. 9th. Divl. Signals for necessary communications until arrival of these H.Q. on 31st July.

8) Acknowledge.

W. G. Micklem[?] Major RE
O.C. 58th DIVISIONAL SIGNAL CO. R.E.

Copy No 1. to Sigs 173 Bde
2 " " 174 "
3 " " 175 "
4 " " 58th Div Artillery
5 " O i/c H.Q. 58th Divl Signal Co RE.
6 & 7 War Diary
8 File.

Instructions regarding War Diaries and Intelligence Summaries are contained in F. S. Regs., Part II. and the Staff Manual respectively. Title Pages will be prepared in manuscript.

WAR DIARY
or
INTELLIGENCE SUMMARY
(Erase heading not required.)

Army Form C. 2118.

58 Div Signals
Vol 8

Place	Date	Hour	Summary of Events and Information	Remarks and references to Appendices
FOSSEUX	1/8/17		Communication to Inf Bdes. by telephone and sounder as follow:-	
			To 173rd Bde MANIN (through 7.30 pm 31/7/17.)	
			" 174th " BERNEVILLE " 11-0 am -"-	
			" 175th " WARLUS " 11-0 am -"-	
			Through to XVII Corps, telephone and sounder (11-am 31/7/17)	
			Through to HQ 58th Divnl. RA HAUTEVILLE (3 pm. 31/7/17).	[illegible]
"	3/8/17	midnt.	Received wire SW16 from O.C. 3rd Army Signals. Lorry with P.E.L. Set to replace present set, leaves for FOSSEUX 8-0 am 4/8/17.	[illegible]
"	4/8/17	9.40 am	Lorry and P.E.L. Set arrive. Present set disconnected and proceeded to 3rd Army en route for GHQ Wireless Depot.	[illegible]
"	5/8/17	7 pm.	2/Lt. A. H. Tew, 2/6th Battn. London Regt. reports for one month's attachment. (Correspondence ref. X102).	
"	"	6 pm.	16 O.R. from 173rd Inf. Bde. report for Power Buzzer Course of one weeks' duration under 2/LT. G.D. ARDEN.	[illegible]
"	6/8/17	10 am	Original P.E.L. lorry returns from GHQ. fitted with new LISTER P.E.L. Set.	
"	"	2 pm	Emergency P.E.L. Set and lorry returned to GHQ.	[illegible]

2449 Wt. W14957/M90 750,000 1/16 J.B.C. & A. Forms/C.2118/12.

Army Form C. 2118.

Instructions regarding War Diaries and Intelligence Summaries are contained in F. S. Regs., Part II. and the Staff Manual respectively. Title Pages will be prepared in manuscript.

WAR DIARY
or
INTELLIGENCE SUMMARY

(Erase heading not required.)

Place	Date	Hour	Summary of Events and Information	Remarks and references to Appendices
FOSSEUX	6/8/17.	6pm	10 O.R. from R.F.A. Report for Fullerphone Course (one week) under CAPT. J. C. WARRINGTON	
"	"	"	12 O.R. from R.F.A. report for Recruit Signalling Course (6 weeks) under CAPT. W.L. BATESON. Sergt. GODWOOD reports from No. 4 Section as Asst. Instructor.	
"	8/8/17	9am	Course of airline construction and maintenance for cable section reinforcements commenced, under 2/LT. PALMER.	
"	11/8/17	6pm.	First Power Buzzer Course terminates; 16 O.R. return to 173rd Inf Bde.	
"	12/8/17	6pm.	8 O.R. from 174th Inf Bde. and 8 O.R. from 175th Inf. Bde. report for Power Buzzer Course (Second), under 2/LT. G.D. ARDEN.	
	13/8/17	6pm	First Fullerphone Course terminates, and 10 O.R. R.F.A. return to Units.	
	14/8/17	9am	Second Fullerphone Course commences, under CAPT. J. C. WARRINGTON, for 12 O.R. of R.F.A. Units.	
	19/8/17	4pm	58th Division Warning Order G.S. 964/4 received and acknowledged.	
"	19/8/17	9am	Cable Det. under 2/LT. T.E. PALMER dismantles and recovers 2 pair airline route FOSSEUX – HAUTEVILLE, under instructions from XVII Corps	
	20/8/17	7am	Cable Det. under 2/LT. T.E. PALMER proceed to LATTRE-ST-QUENTIN, and clear up lines of XVII Corps in that village.	
	"	6pm.	Second Fullerphone Course terminates; 12 O.R. R.F.A. return to Units.	
	"	"	Second Power Course terminates and 12 O.R. return to Units.	

2449 Wt. W14957/M90 750,000 1/16 J.B.C. & A. Forms/C.2118/12.

Army Form C. 2118.

Instructions regarding War Diaries and Intelligence Summaries are contained in F. S. Regs., Part II. and the Staff Manual respectively. Title Pages will be prepared in manuscript.

WAR DIARY
or
INTELLIGENCE SUMMARY

(Erase heading not required.)

Place	Date	Hour	Summary of Events and Information	Remarks and references to Appendices
FOSSEUX	21-8-17	4 pm	58th Divn. letter Q.579/91 (Secret), received and acknowledged, giving train table, and instructions for move.	
	21-8-17	5 pm.	2/LT. T.E PALMER and 2 O.R. leave for new area to arrange billets etc, entraining at MAROEUIL 8.30 pm.	W.E.h
	22-8-17	4 pm	Orders for move issued.	Apx "A"
	22-8-17	11 pm	58th Divn. Operation Order 52 received and acknowledged.	W.E.h
	24-8-17	9 am.	Advance party of 8 O.R. under 2/Lieut. Hacker leave for rear area by lorry.	
	"	7.45 pm	H.Q. and No.1. Sec. leave by road to entrain at ARRAS.	
	"	11 pm	H.Q. and No. 1 Sec. arrive ARRAS and entrain.	W.E.h
	25-8-17	2.20 am	Depart from ARRAS.	
	"	noon	Arrive GODEWASVELDE and detrain.	
	"	2.30 pm	Leave GODEWASVELDE by road and proceed to A16 c 2.3. Sheet 27 and bivouac, arriving 6.0 pm.	W.E.h

2449 Wt. W14957/M90 750,000 1/16 J.B.C. & A. Forms/C.2118/12.

Army Form C. 2118.

Instructions regarding War Diaries and Intelligence Summaries are contained in F. S. Regs., Part II. and the Staff Manual respectively. Title Pages will be prepared in manuscript.

WAR DIARY
or
INTELLIGENCE SUMMARY
(Erase heading not required.)

Place	Date	Hour	Summary of Events and Information	Remarks and references to Appendices
A16 C 2.3. ("X" CAMP) Sheet 28.	26/8/17	8am	58th Division Operation Order No. 53 received and acknowledged.	
	27/8/17	11'30am	ADMS. 58th Div. O.O. No. 26 received and acknowledged.	W.G.h.
	27/8/17	8am	Adv. party proceed to Canal Bank (Adv. Divl H.Q. 48th Division) to look over lines, billets etc.	
	"	7pm	C.R.E. 58th Div. O.O. 26 received and acknowledged.	
	28/8/17	8am	Adv. party & stores leave by lorry for Adv. D.H.Q. 48th Div. for duty at Signal Office	W.G.h.
	"	–"–	Signal Order No. 16 issued	Appx B.
	"	2pm	Further advance party leave for Adv. H.Q. 48th Div. including Signal Office relief.	
	29/8/17	9am	Column leaves "X" Camp for "C" camp (A 30 central) arriving 10am.	W.G.h.
	"	11am	Signal Office closed "X" Camp and opened "C" Camp same hour.	
	"	–"–	Through to Adv. H.Q. 58th Division at C 25 d 3.3. phone and sounder.	
	"	11'45am	Through to XVIII. Corps, phone and sounder.	
	"	12'30pm	Through to Left Bde. (174th) at C 25 d cen. phone and sounder.	
	"	5'0pm.	Through to Right Bde. (175th) at C 25 d 2.9	W.G.h.

W. G. [illegible] Major RE
O.C. 58th DIVISIONAL SIGNAL CO. R.E.

2449 Wt. W14957/M90 750,000 1/16 J.B.C. & A. Forms/C.2118/12.

"Appendix A"

Orders for move of H.Q. and No. 1 Section
from FOSSEUX 24-8-17.

MOVE: (1.) H.Q. and No. 1 Section will move from FOSSEUX to the Fifth Army Area on 24th inst.

TRANSPORT (2). In addition to 1st. line transport the following lorries will be available.

		Destination
2 3-ton lorries report 6 am 24th inst.		New Area.
1 30-cwt. lorry	9 am — " —	ARRAS

ADVANCE-PARTY (3) An advance party of 8 O.R. under 2/Lpl Stocker will leave on one of the first named lorries above, with technical equipment, etc. to open Divisional Office on arrival in new Area. They will be provided with rations up to 25th. inst. midnight.

PARADES (4) Following time table will be observed from 4'30 pm 24th inst:—

24th. inst.	4'30 pm	Tea.
	5'15 pm	Water & feed horses
	7'45 pm.	Parade in full marching order ready to move off.
	10'45 pm.	ARRAS Station arrive
25th. inst.	1'54 am.	-do- -do- depart
	9'54 am	Arrive detraining station.

ENTRAINING ORDERS (5.)(A) Lt. A.H. TEW will proceed in advance of the Unit and will report to the Entraining Officer, line 11, ARRAS station not later than 10'35 pm. taking with him entraining state for the Unit in duplicate

(B) The water cart will be filled before leaving FOSSEUX and will be entrained full. All bottles must be filled before starting.

(C) Horses will be unharnessed, and harness will be laid in the middle of the truck tied up in each man's saddle blanket. Two men will travel in each horse truck and must be detailed by Section N.C.Os. before leaving FOSSEUX.

(D) Picketing ropes will be kept available for use if required. Canvas buckets to accompany horses in the trucks.

SUPPLIES (6.)(A) 2 days rations will be drawn on 23rd inst. for consumption 24th and 25th. Rations for consumption 26th. will be drawn on 24th and carried in Supply Wagon which will accompany the Unit.

SUPPLIES (CONTD) 6. (b) All ranks will, on leaving FOSSEUX, carry on them rations up to midnight 25th inst.

(c). Horses will carry full nose-bags and full haynets. The latter will be given immediately after entrainment, the former retained for use during the journey.

MOTOR CYCLISTS (7) All motor cyclists will proceed by road, 10 leaving at 9am on the 24th. and four at 9am on 25th. inst. The 2 at present attached with H.Q. Divl. Artillery will remain with them and proceed independently.

ELECTRIC LIGHT LORRY (8) Corpl. i/c Electric light lorry will dismantle lights early on the morning of 24th. inst. and proceed by road to new area leaving FOSSEUX not later than 8.30 am.

BILLETS (9) All billets will be cleaned and left in a sanitary condition by 6 pm. 2/LT. ARDEN will inspect same before departure and obtain covering certificate from civilian inhabitants for billets and from Town Major for Military Huts and stables. Any claim made by civilian inhabitants must be made in writing at the time of handing over billets.

DETRAINING. (10) The Company will detrain at GODEWAERSVELDE and march to Divl. H.Q. at A 30 b 2.3. (Sheet 28) via ABEELE. 200 yds. between Companies will be maintained.

D. G. Richelmore
Major RE
O.C. 58th DIVISIONAL SIGNAL CO. R.E.

Copies for
O.C.
Sergt Watson
CSM
FILE (2)

Issued 4 pm 22/8/17.

58th DIVISIONAL SIGNAL Co. R.E.

Appx "B"

Signal Order No. 16 — 28/8/17.

(1) The 58th Division will relieve the 48th Division in the line at 11am on 29th inst. at which hour command passes to G.O.C. 58th Division.

H.Q. (2) Adv. Divl. H.Q. will be at C 25 d 3.3.
Rear [illegible] A 30 central (BRAKE CAMP)

CAMPS (3) [illegible] Signal Coy. will be quartered as follows:—
Office staff and M.Cn. — Adv. Divl. H.Q.
[illegible] and ½ transport (under [illegible]) REIGERSBURG CAMP.
½ transport (under [illegible]) Rear Divl. H.Q.

RELIEF (4) [illegible] will be responsible for relief of Signal Office [illegible] [illegible] [illegible] and [illegible] [illegible] [illegible] Rank. [illegible] will [illegible] [illegible] instruments [illegible] personnel [illegible] [illegible] 2 [illegible] operators per each wireless set and one wireless operator per [illegible] station. All instruments will be taken over in [illegible] as far as possible.

TRANSPORT (5) [illegible] Company Transport will parade under [illegible] in [illegible] marching order to leave "X" Camp at 9am 29th inst. and [illegible] [illegible] personnel to BRAKE CAMP (A 30 central) at Divl. Rear H.Q. There all transport will be left with exception of one [illegible] wagon and [illegible] team 2 limbers and [illegible] teams and the water cart, which, with four riders will proceed to and [illegible] [illegible] REIGERSBURG CHATEAU. Personnel will proceed [illegible] detailed separately.

REAR PARTY (6) [illegible] will [illegible] at Divl. H.Q. until 11am when he will close the Office, [illegible] all local [illegible] and bring same in limber to REIGERSBURG CAMP. All circuits and locals must be [illegible] clearly labelled at both ends. Bells will also be dismantled where installed. On passing BRAKE CAMP he will see that "A" Staff Office has a phone and is connected to the exchange, likewise the A.Q.M.S.

ELECTRIC LIGHT. (7) [illegible] will dismantle lights at "X" Camp and proceed with lorry to BRAKE CAMP where he will install lights as directed by 2/Lt. ARDEN. He will then hand over lighting set to [illegible], and himself report at REIGERSBURG CAMP for duty.

Issued at [illegible] to
[illegible]
Officers Mess
[illegible]
| Diary (2) ✓

W. G. [illegible]
MAJOR, R.E.
O.C. 58th DIVISIONAL SIGNAL CO. R.E.

Instructions regarding War Diaries and Intelligence Summaries are contained in F. S. Regs., Part II. and the Staff Manual respectively. Title Pages will be prepared in manuscript.

WAR DIARY
or
INTELLIGENCE SUMMARY

(Erase heading not required.)

Army Form C. 2118.

58 D Signal Coy

Vol 9

Place	Date	Hour	Summary of Events and Information	Remarks and references to Appendices
"6" Camp A 30 d 0 0 Sheet 28	4/9/17	4pm	O.i/c Signals and Signal personnel of 58th Divl Artillery H.Q. arrive at "6" Camp and take over from 23rd Divisional Artillery Signals.	
	"	8am	Draft of 6 O.R. Reinforcements report from Signal Depot.	
	"	4pm	2/Lieut. T. O. BALK reports from Fifth Army as Supernumerary Officer.	W.G.
	5/9/17	9pm	Forward 6-foot Bury commenced from MOUSETRAP RIDGE to STEENBEEK. 200 men of 174th Bde. commence digging at MOUSETRAP	
	6/9/17	9am	58th Div. Operation Order 54 received and acknowledged.	
	6/9/17	9pm	Bury continued. 200 men of 174th Bde. digging from MOUSETRAP complete 300 yards at average depth, 5'6". 200 men of 175th Bde. digging from STEENBEEK complete 300 yards of trench at an average depth of 5'6".	W.G.
	7/9/17	9pm	200 men of 174th Bde. continue digging from MOUSETRAP and 100 of 175th Bde. from STEENBEEK.	
	8/9/17	–"–	– Ditto –	
	9/9/17	9pm	Working party from 173rd Inf. Bde. commence work on 900 yard trench to connect up with 174th and 175th parties on bury.	W.G.
	"	"		
	10-9-17	5'30pm	Signal Order No. 17 issued.	Apdx "A".
	"	"	Diagram of Signal communications prepared.	Apdx "B" W.G.

2449 Wt. W14957/M90 750,000 1/16 J.B.C. & A. Forms/C.2118/12.

Army Form C. 2118.

Instructions regarding War Diaries and Intelligence Summaries are contained in F. S. Regs., Part II. and the Staff Manual respectively. Title Pages will be prepared in manuscript.

WAR DIARY
or
INTELLIGENCE SUMMARY

(Erase heading not required.)

Place	Date	Hour	Summary of Events and Information	Remarks and references to Appendices
"B" Camp (A30d00. Sheet 28)	11/9/17	2 pm	2/LT. C. MIESEGAES reports from Fifth Army, and proceeds to 290th Bde. R.F.A. as Signal Officer 3/6 Bde Subsection.	W.G.A.
	12/9/17	6pm.	Relief of Signals in connection with Signal Order No. 17 complete.	
	13/9/17	9pm–6am	Bury completed. Final report "Digging light, water interfered with depth of trench; 6'0" obtained in most places, minimum depth 4'6"."	
			58th. Divsl. "Instructions Nos 2 and 3 received and acknowledged.	W.G.A.
	15/9/17	4pm		
	16/9/17	4pm	2/LT. A.H. TEW, 2/6th Battn London Regt, rejoins his Unit on completion of attachment.	W.G.A.
	17/9/17	9.30am	58th Divn. G.S. 1023/77/9-10, Instructions 5 and 6 received and acknowledged.	
	"	3pm	" " Instructions 7 & 8 received and ackgd.	
	"	"	" " Operation Order 56 received and ackgd.	
	18/9/17	noon	58th Divn. Operation Order 57 received and ackgd.	W.G.A.
	17/9/17	mdnt	Signal Office traffic at Divsl. H.Q. for 17/9/17:– Telegrams 755, DR.L.S. 763 Total 1518	
	19/9/17	2pm	Signal Office reliefs leave "B" Camp for Canal Bank.	
CANAL BANK C25d 3.3.	"	6pm	Signal Office opened at CANAL BANK.	
	"	mdnt	Adv. H.Q. Signal Office traffic for 19/9/17 Telegrams 792, DR.L.S 747, Total 1539.	W.G.A.
	20/9/17	5.40 am	ZERO hour.	
	18/9/17	mdnt	Adv. H.Q. Signal Office traffic for 18/9/17, Telegrams 883 DR.L.S 796 total 1679.	W.G.A.

2449 Wt. W14957/M90 750,000 1/16 J.B.C. & A. Forms/C.2118/12.

Army Form C. 2118.

WAR DIARY
or
INTELLIGENCE SUMMARY
(Erase heading not required.)

Instructions regarding War Diaries and Intelligence Summaries are contained in F. S. Regs., Part II. and the Staff Manual respectively. Title Pages will be prepared in manuscript.

Place	Date	Hour	Summary of Events and Information	Remarks and references to Appendices
CANAL BANK	20/9/17	11'30 am	Forward bury blown out by shellfire. 10 pairs out of 30 left working. Traffic diverted to 10 undamaged pairs, and communication uninterrupted on all important circuits.	
	"	9 am	58th Dwsl. Operation Order received and ackgd.	
	"	3'30 pm	Forward bury repaired and lines working O.K.	
	"	9 pm	Signal Order No. 19 issued.	Appx. C
	"	mdnt.	Adv. DHQ Signal Office traffic for the day, Telegrams 1142, DRLS 852, total 1994	
	21/9/17	mdnt	Adv HQ Sig Office traffic for previous 24 hours:- Telegrams 857, DRLS. 779 Total 1636	W. G[illegible]
	25/9/17	8'0 pm	58 Dwsl O.O. 60 received & acknowledged, ordering relief of 58th Div. (less Artillery) by 48th Div. on night of Sept. 27/28.	W. G[illegible]
	26/9/17	9'30 pm	Signal Order No. 20 issued.	Appx. D
	27/9/17	10 am	Advance party leave CANAL BANK to entrain at BRIELEN.	W. G[illegible]
	28/9/17	10 am	Signal Office closed at CANAL BANK. HQ and No. 1 Section proceed to BROWNE CAMP.	W. G[illegible]
BROWNE CAMP	29/9/17	9 am	Transport leaves BROWNE CAMP, proceeds to WORMHOUDT en route for ZUTKERQUE	
	28/9/17		Signal Office for new area established at COCOVE CHAU. (NR. RECQUES)	W. G[illegible]

2449 Wt. W14957/M90 750,000 1/16 J.B.C. & A. Forms/C.2118/12.

Army Form C. 2118.

WAR DIARY
or
INTELLIGENCE SUMMARY
(Erase heading not required.)

Instructions regarding War Diaries and Intelligence Summaries are contained in F. S. Regs., Part II. and the Staff Manual respectively. Title Pages will be prepared in manuscript.

Place	Date	Hour	Summary of Events and Information	Remarks and references to Appendices
ZUTKERQUE	30/9/17	4pm	Column arrives ZUTKERQUE; Camp and wagon lines established.	
"	"		Communications at Signal Office COCOVE CHAU. :-	
			Telephone, Sounder superimposed, to	
			173rd Bde at NORDAUSQUES	
			174th " " LICQUES	
			175th " " NIELLES.	
			XIX Corps " EPERLECQUES.	
"	"		Public Call Office (Officers only) established at Officers' Mess	
			ZUTKERQUE	

[signature] Major R.E.
O.C. 58th DIVISIONAL SIGNAL CO. R.E.

2449 Wt. W14957/M90 750,000 1/16 J.B.C. & A. Forms/C.2118/12.

58th DIVISIONAL
SIGNAL Co. R.E.

Apdx "A"

5.

Signal Order No. 17.

1). 173rd Inf. Bde. will relieve the 174 and 175 Inf. Bdes. in the line on 12/13th Sept. command of Sector passing to Brig-Gen. Cmdg. 173rd. Bde. on completion of relief.

2). O. i/c., Signals 174th. Bde. will take over Signal Office at DAMBRE CAMP from O. i/c. Signals 173rd. Bde. who in his turn will take over Signal Officer at CANAL BANK from O. i/c Signals 175th Bde. Offices will be left fully wired and instruments taken over by mutual arrangement between Signal Officers concerned.

10-line cordless exchanges will be disposed of as follows:-

173 Bde. hands one to 174 Bde. at DAMBRE CAMP
175 " " " " 173 " " CANAL BANK
174 " " " " 175 " for erection in the latters new office.

3) Sigs 173 Bde. will arrange to relieve power buzzer personnel of 174 and 175 Bdes. on all stations on night of 12/13th. in time to enable relieved men to return before dawn.

4). Signals 174 Bde. will take over all local deliveries of telegrams, packets etc. round DAMBRE CAMP from Signals 173 Bde., so that there is no closing of the DAMBRE Office during the relief.

5). Signals 173 Bde. will obtain full lists of men attached for rations to the two outgoing Bdes. and ensure that these men are taken on his strength and supplied with rations from 13th. inst. inclusive.

6). Signals 175 Bde. will report on arrival at BRAKE CAMP to the Divsl. Signal Office for information as to lines etc. to his H.Q.

7). Maintenance of communications on the double Bde. front will be undertaken by No. 2 Section & H.Q. Section Divsl. Signal Coy. Any constructional work for 174 and 175 Bdes. still requiring to be done after the relief is effected must be carried out by the Bde. Signal Officer concerned.

8). Acknowledge.

Issued to —

1. Signals 173 Bde.
2. " 174 "
3. " 175 "
4 " UZZR.
5 & 6. War Diary. ✓
7. File.

[signature]
Major R.E.
O.C. 58th DIVISIONAL SIGNAL CO. R.E.

Issued 8.30pm
Sept. 10/17.

Apdx B

58TH (LON) DIVN.

SIGNAL COMMUNICATIONS

SCALE 1/20,000.

8 58 Div Signals Army Form C. 2118.

Vol 10

Instructions regarding War Diaries and Intelligence Summaries are contained in F. S. Regs., Part II. and the Staff Manual respectively. Title Pages will be prepared in manuscript.

WAR DIARY or INTELLIGENCE SUMMARY

(Erase heading not required.)

Place	Date	Hour	Summary of Events and Information	Remarks and references to Appendices
ZUTKERQUE	1/10/17		During period in rest, syllabus of training issued to include special Classes of Instruction as follow:-	
			(1) Cable Jointing and Airlinemen's Duties (under 2/Lt. PALMER).	
			(2) Wireless and Amplifier (under LT. ARDEN)	
			(3). Office Telegraphists (selected from Wireless Operators) under Signalmaster.	
			(4). Visual (under 2/Lt. BALK)	W.R.J.
	4/10/17	8am	8 O.R. despatched for Fifth Army School, Linemen's Course.	W.R.J.
	7/10/17	9am	8 O.R. despatched to Fifth Army Rest Camp.	
	—"—	—"—	3 O.R. despatched to Fifth Army School for Wireless Course.	W.R.J.
	20/10/17		HQ and No. 1 Sections move from ZUTKERQUE to POPERINGHE	W.R.J.
POPERINGHE	22/10/17	11.40pm	58th Divl. Operation Order 62 received and acknowledged.	
	23/10/17	10am	O.C. Signals wounded at Canal Bank, + removed to C.C.S. PROVEN night of 23/10/17.	W.R.J.
	—"—	8.30pm	58th Divn. O.O. 63 received and acknowledged.	
	24/10/17		Advance parties proceed to Canal Bank, (Adv. DHQ) and Border Camp (Rear DHQ) preparatory to taking over from 18th Division.	W.R.J.

2449 Wt. W14957/M90 750,000 1/16 J.B.C. & A. Forms/C.2118/12.

Army Form C. 2118.

Instructions regarding War Diaries and Intelligence Summaries are contained in F. S. Regs., Part II. and the Staff Manual respectively. Title Pages will be prepared in manuscript.

WAR DIARY
or
INTELLIGENCE SUMMARY

(Erase heading not required.)

Place	Date	Hour	Summary of Events and Information	Remarks and references to Appendices
CANAL BANK C 19. c 3.2.	25/10/17		Remainder of Company move to Canal Bank and Border Camp. 173rd Inf. Bde. relieve 54th Inf. Bde. in the line on night 24/25 Oct., and remain under orders of G.O.C. 58th Division until 10 am 25/10/17.	
	— " —	10 am	Command of Divisional Sector passes to G.O.C. 58th Division.	
	26/10/17	7 pm	58th Div. O.O. 64 received and acknowledged.	W.R.J.
	27/10/17	mdnt	Divl. Signal Office traffic for past 24 hours – Telegrams 709, DRLS 538 Total 1247.	W.R.J.
	28/10/17	8 am	174th Inf. Bde. complete relief of 173rd Inf. Bde in the line.	W.R.J.
	— " —	7 pm	58th Divn. O.O. 65 received and acknowledged.	
	— " —	mdnt	Divl. Signal Office traffic for 24 hours. Telegrams 766. DRLS 569. Total 1335.	
	30/10/17	7.30 pm	58th Divn. O.O. 66 received and acknowledged.	W.R.J.
	30/10/17	mdnt	Divl. Signal Office traffic for 24 hours, Telegrams 756, DRLS. 480, Total 1236.	W.R.J.
	30/10/17	noon	CAPT. O.P. EDGCUMBE reports for duty and assumes command of 58th Divl. Signal Co. RE. vice MAJOR. W.G. MICHELMORE.	W.R.J.

W. R. [illegible] Capt. for
O.C. 58th DIVISIONAL SIGNAL CO. R.E.

2449 Wt. W14957/M90 750,000 1/16 J.B.C. & A. Forms/C.2118/12.

7

Instructions regarding War Diaries and Intelligence Summaries are contained in F. S. Regs., Part II. and the Staff Manual respectively. Title Pages will be prepared in manuscript.

WAR DIARY
or
INTELLIGENCE SUMMARY
(Erase heading not required.)

Army Form C. 2118.

58 D Signal
Vol 11

Place	Date	Hour	Summary of Events and Information	Remarks and references to Appendices
CANAL BANK C19c 3.2	1/11/17		New bury from PHEASANT FARM to NORFOLK HQ. started. 100 men under LT. BALK and LT. HARDY.	W.R.J.
	2/11/17		Division comes under command of II Corps.	W.R.J.
	3/11/17		New bury continued. Unable to get 7-pair lead up, bury accordingly completed with armoured quad.	W.R.J.
	4/11/17.		Bury continued. Old bury across STEENBEEK blown up three times.	W.R.J.
	5/11/17		Bury work continued. New switch from GW-M.W. surveyed.	W.R.J.
	6/11/17		Bury to NORFOLK HQ. finished. 20 pairs through. New switch bury started.	W.R.J.
	7/11/17		Half of first section dug, under supervision of 2/LT. PALMER.	W.R.J.
	8/11/17		First section finished under CAPT. WARRINGTON. 174 Inf. Bde. relieves 175 Inf. Bde in the line.	W.R.J.
	10/11/17		Second section of bury started. No bury work possible on 9/12/17.	W.R.J.
	11/11/17		Second section to GZ. finished.	W.R.J.

2449 Wt. W14957/M90 750,000 1/16 J.B.C. & A. Forms/C.2118/12.

Army Form C. 2118.

Instructions regarding War Diaries and Intelligence Summaries are contained in F. S. Regs., Part II. and the Staff Manual respectively. Title Pages will be prepared in manuscript.

WAR DIARY
or
INTELLIGENCE SUMMARY
(Erase heading not required.)

Place	Date	Hour	Summary of Events and Information	Remarks and references to Appendices
CANAL BANK C19c 3.2.	12/11/17		Third section of bury started.	W.R.J.
	13/11/17		Third section dug, but not sufficient cable for finishing. Capt. O.P. EDGCUMBE wounded and evacuated to C.C.S.	W.R.J.
	14/11/17		Bury finished. New route across STEENBEEK in old bury prospected. No working parties available.	W.R.J.
	15/11/17		30 pairs to GV OK. 20 pairs to GZ.	W.R.J.
	16/11/17		20 pairs tested OK. to M.W. (SNIPE HQ)	
	"		174th Inf Bde. relieved in line.	W.R.J.
	17/11/17		Advance party of 35th. Division arrive. Second-in-Command of Signal Coy shown over Area.	W.R.J.
	"		Lieut. RIDLEY retesting pairs in new switch. 28 pairs through to G.Z.	
	"	10am	Division relieved in line by 35th Div. at 10am. H.Q. at BORDER CAMP close same hour.	W.R.J.
PROVEN.	"	"	D.H.Q. opens at PROVEN. Through to I. Corps. 173 & 175 Inf. Bdes on phone and sounder.	W.R.J.
	18/11/17		174 Inf. Bde. on phone. Sounder superimposed.	W.R.J.

2449 Wt. W14957/M90 750,000 1/16 J.B.C. & A. Forms/C.2118/12.

Instructions regarding War Diaries and Intelligence Summaries are contained in F. S. Regs., Part II. and the Staff Manual respectively. Title Pages will be prepared in manuscript.

WAR DIARY
or
INTELLIGENCE SUMMARY
(Erase heading not required.)

Army Form C. 2118.

Place	Date	Hour	Summary of Events and Information	Remarks and references to Appendices
PROVEN	24/11/17		Advance party sent to NIELLES-LES-BLEQUIN to take over from 5th Division.	WRJ
	25/11/17	11am	D.H.Q. closes PROVEN reopening NIELLES-LES-BLEQUIN same hour. Through to XVIII. Corps on sounder only, and 173 Inf. Bde.	WRJ
	26/11/17		174 Inf. Bde. on phone to Divn. with 173rd. Inf. Bde. on 174th. Bde. exchange. Superimposed to 173 Bde. through 174 Bde.	WRJ
	27/11/17		175th Bde. on phone with sounder superimposed. Working sounder to 173 Bde. with 174th. intermediate.	WRJ

W. R. Jackson Capt/for
O.C. 58th DIVISIONAL SIGNAL CO. R.E.

2449 Wt. W14957/M90 750,000 1/16 J.B.C. & A. Forms/C.2118/12.

Instructions regarding War Diaries and Intelligence Summaries are contained in F. S. Regs., Part II. and the Staff Manual respectively. Title Pages will be prepared in manuscript.

WAR DIARY
or
INTELLIGENCE SUMMARY

(Erase heading not required.)

Army Form C. 2118.

58 D Signals

Vol 12

Place	Date	Hour	Summary of Events and Information	Remarks and references to Appendices
NIELLES-LES-BLEQUIN	4/12/17	2pm	58th Divn. Operation Order 73 received: 58th. Divn. to relieve 35th Divn. in left Sector II Corps front, on night Dec. 8/9th.	
"	5/12/17	7.30am	First Advance party (linesmen etc) leave for Canal Bank to make preliminary arrangements for taking over lines, Test points etc. 2/Lt. PALMER i/c. Party proceeds by Bus.	
"	"	8am.	Second Advance party proceed by lorry to CANAL BANK to arrange transfer of exchanges, instruments etc.	
"	7/12/17	8am	Column and Transport, H.Q and No.1 Section leave NIELLES for WELSH FARM via LEDERZEELE and ST. JAN TER BIEZEN	
"	8/12/17	9am	Two three-ton lorries, with Stores, Signal Office relief etc leave NIELLES for CANAL BANK, and WELSH FARM.	
"	9/12/17	7am	Divnl. H.Q. closes at NIELLES opens at CANALBANK 10am	
"	"	8am	Rear party with last Signal Office relief leave NIELLES by lorry.	
"	"	3pm	Column and transport arrive WELSH FARM.	
CANAL BANK C19 C 3.2.	"	6am	175th Inf. Bde. relieve 105th Inf. Bde. in line.	

[illegible signature] Major, O.C. 58 Divn Signal Coy.

2449 Wt. W14957/M90 750,000 1/16 J.B.C. & A. Forms/C.2118/12.

Army Form C. 2118.

Instructions regarding War Diaries and Intelligence Summaries are contained in F. S. Regs., Part II. and the Staff Manual respectively. Title Pages will be prepared in manuscript.

WAR DIARY
or
INTELLIGENCE SUMMARY
(Erase heading not required.)

Place	Date	Hour	Summary of Events and Information	Remarks and references to Appendices
CANAL BANK C19c 3.2.	14/12/17		Preliminary arrangements for Divisional Signal School discussed with "Q" Staff. Proposed sight DIRTY BUCKET CAMP.	
	15/12/17		Signal School arranged at "G" Camp (A.16.a 9.0). Proceeded to "G" Camp to arrange accommodation and other details.	
	16/12/17	9am	Signal School opens. LIEUT. T.O. BALK i/c.	
	17/12/17	6am	173rd. Inf. Bde. relieve 175th Inf. Bde. in the line. Signal relief completed at 9.30 am.	
	"	noon	LIEUT. G.D. ARDEN wounded. Conveyed to No 64 C.C.S. same day.	
	19/12/17	8.30am	Work commenced on overland route from KEMPTON PARK to A Dugout and W.T. via BW. test point. Party from 174th. Bde. Signal Section assisting.	
	25/12/17	6am	175th Inf. Bde relieve 173rd. Inf. Bde in line.	
	25/12/17		Arrangements completed for Officers Course to be held at Divisl. Signal School, commencing 28th inst.	
	29/12/17	3pm	Divisl. Operation Order 82 received, ordering relief of 175th Inf. Bde. by 173rd. Inf. Bde. in the line. To be completed by 6.30 pm. Jan 1/18.	

J. M. [illegible] [illegible] O.C. 58 [illegible] [illegible]

2449 Wt. W14957/M90 750,000 1/16 J.B.C. & A. Forms/C.2118/12.

Army Form C. 2118.

Instructions regarding War Diaries and Intelligence Summaries are contained in F. S. Regs., Part II. and the Staff Manual respectively. Title Pages will be prepared in manuscript.

WAR DIARY
or
INTELLIGENCE SUMMARY
(Erase heading not required.)

Place	Date	Hour	Summary of Events and Information	Remarks and references to Appendices
CANAL BANK C19c 3.2.	30/12/17	8am	LIEUT. WALKER reports for duty from II. CORPS.	

[illegible signature] Lieut
[illegible] Sig Coy.

2449 Wt. W14957/M90 750,000 1/16 J.B.C. & A. Forms/C.2118/12.

Army Form C. 2118.

Instructions regarding War Diaries and Intelligence Summaries are contained in F. S. Regs., Part II. and the Staff Manual respectively. Title Pages will be prepared in manuscript.

WAR DIARY
or
INTELLIGENCE SUMMARY
(Erase heading not required.)

58 D Signals
Vol 13

Place	Date	Hour	Summary of Events and Information	Remarks and references to Appendices
CANAL BANK C.19.c. 3.2	1/1/18	10am	Conference with A.D. Signals Second Corps, at "J" Sap. Discussed proposed schemes for buries in Divsl. area.	WhJ
	"	6.30pm	173rd Inf. Bde. complete relief of 175th Inf. Bde in the line.	WhJ
	5/1/18	9pm	Divsl. Op. Order 84 received and acknowledged. Relief of 58th Divn. by 35th Divn. to commence 7/1/18 and be completed by 10am 9/1/18. 58th Divn. moves to PROVEN AREA with D.H.Q. at COUTHOVE CHATEAU	WhJ
	6/1/18	mdnt.	Traffic for today at Advanced Divsl. H.Q. Signal Office:— Telegrams 611. D.R.L.S. 844 Total 1455.	WhJ
	8/1/18	9am	Advance party despatched to Couthove Chau.	WhJ
	"	3pm	173rd Inf. Bde. relieved at VARNA FM. by 104th Inf. Bde.	WhJ
	9/1/18	10am	Closed at CANAL BANK. Reopened COUTHOVE CHAU. same hour. H.Q. and No1 sections move by road from CANAL BANK and WELSH FARM to CAMP near COUTHOVE CHAU.	WhJ

2449 Wt. W14957/M90 750,000 1/16 J.B.C. & A. Forms/C.2118/12.

Army Form C. 2118.

WAR DIARY
or
INTELLIGENCE SUMMARY
(Erase heading not required.)

Instructions regarding War Diaries and Intelligence Summaries are contained in F. S. Regs., Part II. and the Staff Manual respectively. Title Pages will be prepared in manuscript.

Place	Date	Hour	Summary of Events and Information	Remarks and references to Appendices
COUTHOVE CHAU.	15/1/18	6pm	Admin. Instns. re move of 58 Divn. to Fifth Army received and acknowledged.	[illegible]
"	17/1/18	2pm	58th Div. O.O. 87 received and ackgd. (re move of Divn. to BOVES AREA on 20/1/18).	[illegible]
"	19/1/18	8am	Advance party despatched, by lorry to CORBIE.	[illegible]
"	20/1/18	8am	Closed at COUTHOVE CHAU. Reopened same hour at CORBIE.	[illegible]
"	"	9.30pm	H.Q. and No 1 Sec. entrained at PROVEN.	
CORBIE	21/1/18	11am	Arrived VILLERS BRETONNEUX, detrained and proceeded by road to CORBIE.	[illegible]
"	22/1/18	1pm	through to 174th Inf. Bde. at MOREUIL.	
"	"	4.30pm	" " 173rd " " " FORT MANOIR	[illegible]
"	24/1/18	5pm	Cable detachment despatched to H.Q. 58th Divsl. Artillery	[illegible]
"	26/1/18	3pm	58th Divsl Arty Group Orders 87 and 88 received, re relief of French Artillery on front of 30th Divn. 30/1/18 – 1/2/18.	[illegible]

2449 Wt. W14957/M90 750,000 1/16 J.B.C. & A. Forms/C.2118/12.

Army Form C. 2118.

Instructions regarding War Diaries and Intelligence Summaries are contained in F. S. Regs., Part II. and the Staff Manual respectively. Title Pages will be prepared in manuscript.

WAR DIARY
or
INTELLIGENCE SUMMARY

(Erase heading not required.)

Place	Date	Hour	Summary of Events and Information	Remarks and references to Appendices
CORBIE	26/1/18	8am	Cable detachment despatched to H.Q. 30th Division.	[illegible]
	"	10am	Signals 58th Divl. Arty close ERCHEU	
	"	4pm	" " " " reopen at CHAUNY.	
	29/1/18	noon	Through to Fifth Army in place of III Corps	[illegible]
	30/1/18	9.30am	174th Inf. Bde. close at MOREUIL and reopen same hour at BERTEAUCOURT.	[illegible]

[illegible signature] Capt RE
for O.C. 58th DIVISIONAL SIGNAL CO. R.E

2449 Wt. W14957/M90 750,000 1/16 J.B.C. & A. Forms/C.2118/12.

Instructions regarding War Diaries and Intelligence Summaries are contained in F. S. Regs., Part II. and the Staff Manual respectively. Title Pages will be prepared in manuscript.

WAR DIARY
or
INTELLIGENCE SUMMARY
(Erase heading not required.)

Army Form C. 2118.

58 D Signals
Vol 14

Place	Date	Hour	Summary of Events and Information	Remarks and references to Appendices
CORBIE	1/2/18	6pm	Airline route from BERTEAUCOURT to MOREUIL completed.	
"	4/2/18	2pm	Divisional O.O. 88 ordering relief of 30th Divn. by 58th Divn. in Southern Sector of III Corps front, to be completed by noon 9/2/18.	
"	Feb. 2-4. 1918.		Cable Det. repairing permanent route between BRAY and CORBIE (for Fifth Army).	
"	6/2/18	8'30 am	Advance party despatched to ROUEZ.	
"	7/2/18	8am	H.Q. and No. 1 Section transport leave for ROUEZ via BUCHOIR and BUSSY arrive ROUEZ. D.H.Q. closes CORBIE and reopens ROUEZ.	
ROUEZ	9/2/18	noon	Rear party depart from CORBIE by lorry.	
	"	1pm	" " arrive ROUEZ.	
ROUEZ	11/2/18	9am	Commenced construction of semi-permanent 2-pair route ROUEZ to SENCENY. (One pair Divn. to Bde. one pair Divsl Arty to Bde.)	
"	15/2/18	6pm	Above route completed, and lateral permanent line SINCENY — QUESSY commenced.	
	19/2/18	—	Completed SINCENY — QUESSY line.	
	20/2/18	9am 6pm	Working party patrolling and regulating Divisional routes.	
	23/2/18	9'15am	Divsl. O.O. 89 received and acknowledged.	

GmA

2449 Wt. W14957/M90 750,000 1/16 J.B.C. & A. Forms/C.2118/12.

Instructions regarding War Diaries and Intelligence Summaries are contained in F. S. Regs., Part II. and the Staff Manual respectively. Title Pages will be prepared in manuscript.

WAR DIARY
or
INTELLIGENCE SUMMARY
(Erase heading not required.)

Army Form C. 2118.

Place	Date	Hour	Summary of Events and Information	Remarks and references to Appendices
ROUEZ	23/2/18	9pm	C.R.E's O.O. 33 received and acknowledged.	
"	24/2/18	2pm	58 Divsl. OO 90 received and acknowledged.	
"	25/2/18	8am	Advance party (of Cable Section) proceed to QUIERZY	
"	—"—	2pm	Additional line constructed on existing route ROUEZ – VILLEQUIER AUMONT.	
"	27/2/18	9.30 am	H.Q. and No. 1 Section move to QUIERZY.	
"	27/2/18	10am	Closed at ROUEZ and re-opened at QUIERZY same hour.	

[signature] Lt Col
O.C. 58th DIVISIONAL SIGNAL Co. R.E.

2449 Wt. W14957/M90 750,000 1/16 J.B.C. & A. Forms/C.2118/12.

7 Army Form C. 2118. 58

WAR DIARY
or
INTELLIGENCE SUMMARY

(Erase heading not required.)

58 D Signals Vol 15

Instructions regarding War Diaries and Intelligence Summaries are contained in F. S. Regs., Part II. and the Staff Manual respectively. Title Pages will be prepared in manuscript.

Place	Date	Hour	Summary of Events and Information	Remarks and references to Appendices
QUIERZY	3/3/18.	9 am.	First stage of Divl Bury commenced at BUTTES DE ROUY (H1.C 93) working towards SINCENY with digging party of 140 O.R. (30 pairs).	
"	4/3/18.	9 am.	Second stage of Divl Bury commenced from Bn H.Q. - H28. b 32. working west. (under Signal Officer 174 Bde).	
"	5/3/18	6 pm.	First stage of Bury completed to Test Point at H 7 c 87 (70 0) Digging party decreased on 4th and 5th to 100.	
"	6/3/18	9 am	After completion of 200 yds of second stage of Bury rock has been encountered about 2 ft. below the surface. Diversion of route considered impracticable. Bury therefore continued in shallow trench for approx 300 yds, when deep trench was again practicable.	
"	7/3/18.	9 am.	First stage of bury continued from H 7 c. 8.7. (70 0) towards SINCENY Digging party 140. Burying 30 - pairs.	
"	9/3/18	6 pm.	First stage bury completed as far as G 12 d 8.5. Led in to test point and terminated temporarily. Second stage bury complete to H 27 a. 2.0. and continued Northward	WM

2449 Wt. W14957/M90 750,000 1/16 J.B.C. & A. Forms/C.2118/12.

Army Form C. 2118.

WAR DIARY
or
INTELLIGENCE SUMMARY

(Erase heading not required.)

Instructions regarding War Diaries and Intelligence Summaries are contained in F. S. Regs., Part II. and the Staff Manual respectively. Title Pages will be prepared in manuscript.

Place	Date	Hour	Summary of Events and Information	Remarks and references to Appendices
QUIERZY.	12/3/18	9 am	Third stage of bury commenced (15 pairs and pilot) from Btn H.Q. at H 3 a 5.3. working in S.E. direction.	
"	16/3/18	6 pm	Second stage of bury completed to H.15.c.2.9. and terminated.	
"	20/3/18	3 pm.	Message "Prepare to attack" received from General Staff 58th Divsn.	
"	21/3/18	5.20 am	Message "Man Battle Stations" received from General Staff 58th Divsn.	
"	21/3/18	4 pm.	Direct line put through to VIRY NOUREUIL in anticipation of move of 173rd Inf. Bde	
"	"	10.30 pm	173rd Inf Bde established at VIRY NOUREUIL	
"	"	"	58th Divsn O.O 92 received and acknowledged.	
"	22/3/18	3 pm	58th Divsn. O.O. 93 received and acknowledged	
"	"	9 pm.	174th Inf Bde move to PIERREMANDE.	
"	"	12 Mdnt.	173rd Inf Bde move to CHAUNY	
"	23/3/18.	Noon.	"Special Instructions" received from General Staff 58th Divsn. Divsn comes under orders of 1st (French) Cavalry Corps.	
"	24/3/18	2.15 am	173rd Inf. Bde. closing at CHAUNY.	
"	"	3.25 am	173rd Inf Bde Signal Office established at ABBECOURT and communication established	
"	"	9.55 am	173rd Inf. Bde. close ABBECOURT.	
"	"	11 am.	Column move QUIERZY to VARESNES.	KRJ

2449 Wt. W14957/M90 750,000 1/16 J.B.C. & A. Forms/C.2118/12.

Instructions regarding War Diaries and Intelligence Summaries are contained in F. S. Regs., Part II. and the Staff Manual respectively. Title Pages will be prepared in manuscript.

WAR DIARY
or
INTELLIGENCE SUMMARY
(Erase heading not required.)

Army Form C. 2118.

Place	Date	Hour	Summary of Events and Information	Remarks and references to Appendices
VARESNES	24/3/18.	11.55am	Divisional Signal Office opened at VARESNES.	
"	"	4pm.	Divisional Signal Office closed at QUIERZY.	
"	"	7pm	Divsnl. O.O. 94 received and acknowledged.	
"	"	7.30pm	Divsnl. Signal Office opened at CAMELIN.	
CAMELIN.	"	"	Column move from VARESNES to CAMELIN.	
"	"	10pm.	Divsnl Signal Office closes at VARESNES.	
"	25/3/18.	4.30pm	Divsnl. O.O. 95 received and acknowledged.	
"	"	11pm.	" " " 96 " " "	
"	26/3/18	12.30pm	" " " 97 " " "	
"	"	5.30pm	Column leave CAMELIN for NAMPCEL.	
"	"	7pm	Move of Column cancelled; return to CAMELIN.	
"	"	9.30pm	Divisional. O.O. 98 received and acknowledged.	
"	27/3/18.	10.am.	Column move CAMELIN to NAMPCEL	
"	"	noon.	Warning order received in reference to relief of 24th (French) Regt.	
"	"	3pm.	Divsnl Signal Office closes at CAMELIN	
BLERANCOURT.	"	"	" " " opens at BLERANCOURT. Through to all Inf Bdes.	

2449 Wt. W14957/M90 750,000 1/16 J.B.C. & A. Forms/C.2118/12.

Army Form C. 2118.

WAR DIARY
or
INTELLIGENCE SUMMARY
(Erase heading not required.)

Instructions regarding War Diaries and Intelligence Summaries are contained in F. S. Regs., Part II. and the Staff Manual respectively. Title Pages will be prepared in manuscript.

Place	Date	Hour	Summary of Events and Information	Remarks and references to Appendices
BLERANCOURT	28/3/18	9.30 am	Column moves from NAMPCEL, halting near AUDIGNICOURT noon to 2 pm. and proceeding to BLERANCOURT, arriving 3.30 p.m.	
"	"	10 pm	Divsnl. O.O 99 received and acknowledged.	
"	29/3/18.	11.30 pm	" . O.O.100. " " "	
"	30/3/18	9 am to 7 pm	Working parties extending all main circuits to alternative position for Divsnl Signal Office in caves at X.2.d.5.2. Sheet 70 E.	
"	31/3/18.	9.30 am to 7. pm.	Working parties completing construction of lines to caves; route constructed from Divsnl Signal Office to proposed Inf. Bde H.Q at ST. AUBIN	

for [signature] Capt RE
O.C. 58th DIVISIONAL SIGNAL CO. R.E.

[initials]

2449 Wt. W14957/M90 750,000 1/16 J.B.C. & A. Forms/C.2118/12.

58th DIVISIONAL SIGNAL COMPANY, R.E.

A P R I L

1 9 1 8

Instructions regarding War Diaries and Intelligence Summaries are contained in F. S. Regs., Part II. and the Staff Manual respectively. Title Pages will be prepared in manuscript.

or

INTELLIGENCE SUMMARY

(Erase heading not required.)

58 D Signals

Vol 16

Place	Date	Hour	Summary of Events and Information	Remarks and references to Appendices
BLERANCOURT	1/4/18	12'15am	58th Divn. Operation Order 101 received and acknowledged.	
		3'30pm	Addendum No.1 to above received.	
		7'30pm	Addendum No.2 to above received. 58th Divn. to be relieved by French 161 and 55 Divns. at 9am 3/4/18. D.H.Q closes BLERANCOURT and reopens SALEUX at that hour.	
		11pm	Administrative Instructions Nos. 1 and 2 ref. O.O. 101 received.	[illegible]
	2/4/18	8am	Advance party, one Signal Office relief leave by lorry for SALEUX	[illegible]
	3/4/18	1pm	Add. No 4 to O.O. 101 received.	
	4/4/18	8am	H.Q and No.1 Sections leave by road for LONGPONT to entrain for new area at midnight 5/6th. halting night of 4th. en route.	[illegible]
	4/4/18	12'30pm	Rear details and Signal Office relief leave by lorry for SALEUX, halting night of 4th at ST. JUST.	[illegible]
	5/4/18	2pm	Rear details etc. arrive SALEUX and proceed to GLISY.	[illegible]
GLISY	"	2'30pm	Divsl. Opor. Order 102 received and acknowledged.	
	"	4pm	Adv. H.Q open at GLISY. Rear H.Q at SALEUX	
	"	10pm	"SY" Cable Section (loaned from III Corps) arrive at GLISY.	[illegible]

2449 Wt. W14957/M90 750,000 1/16 J.B.C. & A. Forms/C.2118/12.

Instructions regarding War Diaries and Intelligence Summaries are contained in F. S. Regs., Part II. and the Staff Manual respectively. Title Pages will be prepared in manuscript.

or

INTELLIGENCE SUMMARY

(Erase heading not required.)

Place	Date	Hour	Summary of Events and Information	Remarks and references to Appendices
GLISY	6/4/18	9am to 5pm	"SY" Cable Section employed on construction of lines between Division and Brigades, returning to III Corps on completion.	KFJ
	7/4/18	7pm	Divsl. Op. Order 103 received and acknowledged.	KFJ
	9/4/18	8am	Cable Det. and office personnel despatched to GENTELLES to open Signal Office of Divsl. R.A.	
		11am	Divsl Op. Order 104 received and acknowledged.	KFJ
	12/4/18	10pm	Divsl. Op. Order 105 received and acknowledged.	
	13/4/18	5 am	Cable Detachment leave to construct lines (1) 175th Inf. Bde. to 174th. Inf. Bde. (2) 174th Inf. Bde. to 39th Divsl. R.A., (3) 174th Inf. Bde. to MR pole, connecting up to existing route and joining through to FORT MANOIR CHAU.	
"		9am	Column moves SALEUX to FORT MANOIR CHAU. also Adv. Divsl. Signal Office from GLISY to same point. Signal Office relief and personnel for Adv. Divsl. Exchange proceed to GENTELLES.	
"		12noon	Divsl. Signal Office closes GLISY and re-opens FORT MANOIR CHAU. same hour.	KFJ

2449 Wt. W14957/M90 750,000 1/16 J.B.C. & A. Forms/C.2118/12.

Instructions regarding War Diaries and Intelligence Summaries are contained in F. S. Regs., Part II. and the Staff Manual respectively. Title Pages will be prepared in manuscript.

or

INTELLIGENCE SUMMARY

(Erase heading not required.)

Place	Date	Hour	Summary of Events and Information	Remarks and references to Appendices
FORT MANOIR CHATEAU	13/4/18	2.30 pm	Divl. Op. Order 106 received and acknowledged.	KLH
	14/4/18	4pm.	Divl. Op Order 107 received and acknowledged.	KLH
	"	mdnt.	Divl Signal Office traffic for the day – Telegrams 820. D.R.L.S. 884 Total 1704.	
	15/4/18	mdnt.	" " " " " " " – Telegrams 756 DRLS. 846 Total 1602	KLH
	17/4/18	noon	Divl. Op. Order 108 received and acknowledged.	
	"	11am	Adv. Divl. Exchange closed at GENTELLES. Personnel return to H.Q.	
	18/4/18	1pm	Divl. Op. Order 109 recd and ackgd.	
	"	mdnt.	Traffic for today Telegrams 749, D.R.L.S. 820 Total 1569. (Special D.Rs. 47)	
	20/4/18	3pm	2/LT. D R. SIMPSON (R.E.T.C) reports from 3rd Corps for duty, Supy. Officer vice LT. HENRY, M.C., gassed, to C.C.S. 18/4/18.	KLH
	21/4/18	mdnt.	Command of left Subsector Divl. front passes to G.O.C. 8th Divn.	KLH

2449 Wt. W14957/M90 750,000 1/16 J.B.C. & A. Forms/C.2118/12.

Instructions regarding War Diaries and Intelligence Summaries are contained in F. S. Regs., Part II. and the Staff Manual respectively. Title Pages will be prepared in manuscript.

or

INTELLIGENCE SUMMARY

(Erase heading not required.)

Place	Date	Hour	Summary of Events and Information	Remarks and references to Appendices
FORT MANOIR CHAU.	22/4/18	1pm	Divl O.O. 110 recd and ackgd.	
	"	10pm	C.R.E. O.O. 40 — " —	[initials]
	23/4/18	9pm	C.R.E. O.O. 41 — " —	
	24/4/18	noon	12 Message Dogs with 4 men report to Bde. in line from 3rd Corps.	[initials]
	26/4/18	4pm	58th Divn. G748 received, ordering relief of Divn. by 165 French Divn in line on night 26-27th.	[initials]
	27/4/18	1am	58th Divn. G764 recd and ackgd. instructions for relief as above.	[initials]
	27/4/18	1pm 8pm	H.Q. & No. 1 Section leave for ST. RICQUIER, lorries direct, transport halting night of 27-28 at CROUY	[initials]
	28/4/18	9am	Divl Signal Office opens at ST. RICQUIER.	
		11am	— " — — " — — " — closes FORT MANOIR. Rear party to ST. RICQUIER by lorry.	[initials]

2449 Wt. W14957/M90 750,000 1/16 J.B.C. & A. Forms/C.2118/12.

or

INTELLIGENCE SUMMARY

(Erase heading not required.)

Instructions regarding War Diaries and Intelligence Summaries are contained in F. S. Regs., Part II. and the Staff Manual respectively. Title Pages will be prepared in manuscript.

Place	Date	Hour	Summary of Events and Information	Remarks and references to Appendices
ST. RICQUIER	28/4/18	1pm	Transport arrives and parks.	[illegible]
"	30/4/18		Preliminary arrangements made for re-opening Signal School at ONEUX. Personnel for classes report ONEUX Church 4-5 pm.	
"	"	9am	Wireless course commenced at ST. RICQUIER	[illegible]

[illegible signature] Capt RE
for O.C. 58th DIVISIONAL SIGNAL CO. R.E.

2449 Wt. W14957/M90 750,000 1/16 J.B.C. & A. Forms/C.2118/12.

7

Instructions regarding War Diaries and Intelligence Summaries are contained in F. S. Regs., Part II. and the Staff Manual respectively. Title Pages will be prepared in manuscript.

WAR DIARY
or
INTELLIGENCE SUMMARY
(Erase heading not required.)

Army Form C. 2118.

58 D Signals

Vol 17

Place	Date	Hour	Summary of Events and Information	Remarks and references to Appendices
ST. RICQUIER	3/5/18	2pm	Memo. 1538 received from G.S. 58th Divn. Preliminary warning orders 58th Divn. to be in reserve on relief of Australian Corps by 3rd Corps. about May 6th.	
	4/5/18	4pm	Operation Order 111 received – orders for above.	
	5/5/18	10am	Wireless demonstration held, and Wireless communication discussed, with Battn and Bde. Signal Officers 174 Bde.	
	"	"	Signal School and Wireless Class join respective Units for move.	
	6/5/18	8'30am	Dismounted party despatched to MOLLIENS-AU-BOIS by bus.	
	"	12noon	Divsl Signal Office closes ST. RIQUIER and opens MOLLIENS-AU-BOIS.	
	7/5/18	10am	Remainder of H.Q. and No. 1 to MOLLIENS-AU-BOIS by lorries.	
MOLLIENS-AU-BOIS	8/5/18	10pm	58th Divsl. Op. Order 112 received and acknowledged.	
	9/5/18	2pm	Wireless Class re-assembles	
	"	5pm	Signal School re-assembles at MIRVAUX	

[signature]

2449 Wt. W14957/M90 750,000 1/16 J.B.C. & A. Forms/C.2118/12.

Army Form C. 2118.

Instructions regarding War Diaries and Intelligence Summaries are contained in F. S. Regs., Part II. and the Staff Manual respectively. Title Pages will be prepared in manuscript.

WAR DIARY
or
INTELLIGENCE SUMMARY
(Erase heading not required.)

Place	Date	Hour	Summary of Events and Information	Remarks and references to Appendices
MOLLIENS-AU-BOIS	11/5/18	7pm	58th Divl. Op. Order 113 received and acknowledged.	
	12/5/18	9am	Work commenced on Corps bury scheme. Working party 290 OR. 2/4th Londons digging from C.11.d.10.7. under 2/LT. PALMER, working towards 175 Bde H.Q. + completing ¼-mile of bury to C.11.b.4.5.	
	13/5/18	9am	Working party as yesterday complete further ¼-mile of bury to 175 Bde H.Q. b17a 8.8.	
	14/5/18	3.30pm	Divl. Op. Order 114 received and acknowledged.	
	15/5/18	5pm	Work on bury from 12th inst. to date consists of 32-pair bury from b.12a 9.6. to pt. 250 yds. W. of Tunnel at b15c 8.4. Joints completed to 175 Bde H.Q. b17a 8.8.	
	16/5/18	9am	Advance party despatched to new Adv. H.Q. near BAISEUX.	
		7pm	Advance party to new Divl. H.Q. CONTAY.	
	17/5/18	9am	H.Q. and No 1 Sec. move to CONTAY.	
CONTAY	"	10am	Divl. Signal Office closes MOLLIENS-AU-BOIS and re-opens CONTAY.	

2449 Wt. W14957/M90 750,000 1/16 J.B.C. & A. Forms/C.2118/12.

Army Form C. 2118.

Instructions regarding War Diaries and Intelligence Summaries are contained in F. S. Regs., Part II. and the Staff Manual respectively. Title Pages will be prepared in manuscript.

WAR DIARY
or
INTELLIGENCE SUMMARY

(Erase heading not required.)

Place	Date	Hour	Summary of Events and Information	Remarks and references to Appendices
CONTAY	20/5/18	8.30pm	58th Division Operation Order 115 received. 173rd Bde relieve 175th Bde. in left Subsector of Divl. front, night May 22-23rd.	
"	24/5/18	8.30am	Bury cable party assisting 47th Divl. Signal Coy. in burying cable from point V25.b.39 working towards BAISEUX.	
"	25/5/18	2.30pm	58th Divn. Operation Order 116 received. 175th Bde. relieve 174th Bde night May 27-28 in Right Subsector.	
"	27/5/18	2.30pm	Divl. Operation Order 117 received and acknowledged.	
"	29/5/18	6am.	24-hour period of suspension of telephone and telegraph forward, commences. Visual stations manned. Mounted D.R. services arranged, and Wireless Station reliefs detailed.	
	30/5/18	1pm	Divl. Operation Order 118 received. Relief of 58th Divn. by 18th Divn. to be completed June 2/18.	
	31/5/18	2pm	All details of Signal relief arranged with O.C. 18th Divl. Signal Co.	

[illegible] Major [illegible]
O.C. 58th DIVISIONAL SIGNAL CO. R.E.

2449 Wt. W14957/M90 750,000 1/16 J.B.C. & A. Forms/C.2118/12.

Army Form C. 2118.

WAR DIARY
or
INTELLIGENCE SUMMARY
(Erase heading not required.)

58 D Signals
Vol 18

Instructions regarding War Diaries and Intelligence Summaries are contained in F. S. Regs., Part II. and the Staff Manual respectively. Title Pages will be prepared in manuscript.

Place	Date	Hour	Summary of Events and Information	Remarks and references to Appendices
CONTAY	1/6/18	7pm	Adv. party despatched to MOLLIENS-AU-BOIS	
	2/6/18	3 am	Divsl. Signal Office opened at —"—	
	"	6 am	H.Q. and No. 1 Section move to —"—	W.L.J.
	"	10am	Closed at CONTAY.	
MOLLIENS-AU-BOIS	3/6/18	9'30am	III Corps Bury scheme continued, 400 O.R. 175 Bde. commence at V 25. c. 2. 8. deepening trench from 3'6" to 6'6"; cable laid and trench filled in as far as V 30 b 5. 0. (¼ mile).	W.L.J.
	4/6/18	7'30am	Working party report at V. 25 c. 2. 8 (175 Bde.) and V 30 a 4. 2. (173 Bde) ¼ mile trench dug, 6'6" deep, cable laid and trench filled in, to V 30 a 4. 2. Further ¼ mile trench dug 4'0" deep to V 29 d 8.9.	W.L.J.
	5/6/18	7'30am	Cable burying continued. Party report V 30 a 4. 2. Trench commenced yesterday deepened, cable laid, + trench filled in.	W.L.J.
	5/6/18	2 pm	Divsl. Op. Order 119 received, ordering moves of Inf. Bdes.	W.L.J.

2449 Wt. W14957/M90 750,000 1/16 J.B.C. & A. Forms/C.2118/12.

Instructions regarding War Diaries and Intelligence Summaries are contained in F. S. Regs., Part II. and the Staff Manual respectively. Title Pages will be prepared in manuscript.

WAR DIARY
or
INTELLIGENCE SUMMARY
(Erase heading not required.)

Army Form C. 2118.

Place	Date	Hour	Summary of Events and Information	Remarks and references to Appendices
MOLLIENS AU BOIS	5/6/18	3pm	LIEUT F.G. BRYANT M.C. proceeds to 4th Army Signal School for duty.	
	8/6/18	8am	LIEUT. WALKER. C.W. despatched for reconnaissance 31st French Corps front.	
	10/6/18	12.40am	Divsl. Op. Order 120 received, ordering move to CAVILLON area.	
	"	4am	Advance party by lorry to CAVILLON	
		6am	Transport leaves for —"—	
		11am	Closed at MOLLIENS AU BOIS	
		3pm	Opened at CAVILLON.	
CAVILLON	14/6/18	11pm	Warning Order G.S. 2061 received, notifying probable relief of 47th Divn June 17-20.	
	15/6/18	9pm	Op. Order 121 recd. ordering above relief	
	17/6/18	2pm	Wireless Section and advance stores to BEAUCOURT by lorries.	
	18/6/18	2pm	Advance party and stores " —"— —"—	
	19/6/18	12.30pm	Dismounted party and stores " —"— —"—	

2449 Wt. W14957/M90 750,000 1/16 J.B.C. & A. Forms/C.2118/12.

Army Form C. 2118.

Instructions regarding War Diaries and Intelligence Summaries are contained in F. S. Regs., Part II. and the Staff Manual respectively. Title Pages will be prepared in manuscript.

WAR DIARY
or
INTELLIGENCE SUMMARY

(Erase heading not required.)

Place	Date	Hour	Summary of Events and Information	Remarks and references to Appendices
CAVILLON	20/6/18	5 am	Transport to BEAUCOURT.	
	"	7 am	Divl. Signal Office at BEAUCOURT and Adv. Office at BAISIEUX taken over from 47th Divn.	
	"	10 am	Closed at CAVILLON. Rear party to BEAUCOURT by lorry.	[illegible]
BEAUCOURT	23/6/18	2 pm	Divl. Op. Order 122 received and acknowledged.	
	"	"	132nd Inf. Regt. (American) establish H.Q. at BEAUCOURT. Communication provided to Divl Signal Office.	[illegible]
	28/6/18	8.30 pm	Divl Operation Order 123 received and acknowledged. (174 Inf Bde. relieve 173 Inf Bde. in left subsector on night 1/2nd July).	[illegible]
	"	9 am – 6 pm	Proposed bury prospected from Right Bde H.Q.	
	29/6/18	2 pm	88th Labour Coy. arrive and take up billets in BAISIEUX. To be employed as working party for Divisional forward bury.	[illegible]
	29/6/18	7 am	Cable Detachment sent forward for work on bury. Billeted at BAISIEUX	[illegible]

2449 Wt. W14957/M90 750,000 1/16 J.B.C. & A. Forms/C.2118/12.

Army Form C. 2118.

Instructions regarding War Diaries and Intelligence Summaries are contained in F. S. Regs., Part II. and the Staff Manual respectively. Title pages will be prepared in manuscript.

WAR DIARY
or
INTELLIGENCE SUMMARY.
(Erase heading not required.)

Place	Date	Hour	Summary of Events and Information	Remarks and references to Appendices
BEAUCOURT	30/4/18	8 am	Work commenced at Right Bde. H.Q. (D.21.b 5.1) on trench for bury. [signature] Major R.E. O.C. 58th DIVISIONAL SIGNAL CO. R.E.	

D. D. & L., London, E.C.
(A10266) Wt W5300/P713 750,000 2/18 Sch. 52 Forms/C2118/16.

"B"

A15/3832

C.R.A.
C.R.E.
~~C.R.E~~
Signals.
173rd Inf. Bde.
174th do
175th do
58th Bn. M.G.C.

4th Suffolks.
Div. Train.
A.D.M.S.
"G"(for information.)

DESTRUCTION OF TELEGRAPH AND TELEPHONE ROUTES.

Under no circumstances are telegraph poles or stay wires to be interfered with, or in any way used in the erection of shelters.

Buries are not to be dug up or cables cut.

The greatest difficulty has been experienced during the late operations through the neglect of these orders, and all cases are to be at once brought to notice and severely dealt with.

It should be pointed out to all ranks that it is most essential to the successful carrying out of the advance that all means of communication should be very carefully guarded and preserved.

Lt-Colonel,
A.A. & Q.M.G. 58th Division.

22/9/18.

Instructions regarding War Diaries and Intelligence Summaries are contained in F. S. Regs., Part II, and the Staff Manual respectively. Title pages will be prepared in manuscript.

WAR DIARY
or
INTELLIGENCE SUMMARY.
(*Erase heading not required.*)

Army Form C. 2118.

58 D Signals
Vol 19

Place	Date	Hour	Summary of Events and Information	Remarks and references to Appendices
BEAUCOURT	1/7/18	3pm	22 O.R. of 33rd American Division report for attachment for instruction in Signal work.	
	2/7/18	7am	2 linemen and 2 office men of American personnel despatched to each Inf. Bde, 2 linemen to Adv Division. Remaining [illegible] employed at Divsl H.Q. in Signal Office, on local routes etc.	
	2/7/18	1pm	Work on bury now completed from Right Bde H.Q. to point of crossing main AMIENS-ALBERT Road, (approx 500 yds).	
	4/7/18	8:30pm	Divsl Op Order 124 received. 173rd Inf Bde relieve 175th in Right Subsector on night of July 6/7th.	
	5/7/18	9am-4pm	Preliminary arrangements made in connection with "Corps silent period" 9am - 7pm July 6th during which time telegraph and telephone circuits will not be used below Corps H.Q. except where specially authorised.	
	6/7/18	9am	Corps Silent period commences. Signal Office traffic diverted to Visual Stations and Wireless.	
	8/7/18	6pm	58 Division G 899 received "Battle Stations Practice".	[signature]

D. D. & L., London, E.C.
(A10266) Wt W5300/P713 750,000 2/18 Sch. 52 Forms/C2118/16.

Army Form C. 2118.

Instructions regarding War Diaries and Intelligence Summaries are contained in F. S. Regs., Part II. and the Staff Manual respectively. Title pages will be prepared in manuscript.

WAR DIARY
or
INTELLIGENCE SUMMARY.
(Erase heading not required.)

Place	Date	Hour	Summary of Events and Information	Remarks and references to Appendices
BEAUCOURT	9/7/18	2pm	Personnel of 33rd American Division return to their Units, having completed period of attachment for instruction.	
	10/7/18	2pm	58 Division G.S. 29 received. 47th Divn. to relieve 8th Divn. in Left Sector on July 13th	
	"	6pm	58 Divn. Op. Order 125 received 175th relieve 174th Inf Bde in Left Subsector on night 12/13th July	
	16/7/18	6pm	58 Divn. Op. Order 126 received. Occupation BAISIEUX System by 132nd. (U.S.) Regt.	
	17/7/18	4pm	58 Divn Op Order 127 received. 174th relieve 173rd. Inf Bde. in Right Subsector on night 18/19th July	
	18/7/18	5pm	58 Divn. Op. Order 128 received, ordering move of 173rd Inf Bde to ROUND WOOD on July 20th 1918	
	21/7/18	2pm	58th Divn Op. Order 129 received, ordering attachment of 132nd. Amer. Regt	
	24/7/18	6pm	58th Divn. Warning Order received (Alteration of Divl. Boundary)	

D. D. & L., London, E.C.
(A10266) Wt W5300/P713 750,000 2/18 Sch. 52 Forms/C2118/16.

Instructions regarding War Diaries and Intelligence Summaries are contained in F. S. Regs., Part II. and the Staff Manual respectively. Title pages will be prepared in manuscript.

WAR DIARY
or
INTELLIGENCE SUMMARY.
(Erase heading not required.)

Army Form C. 2118.

Place	Date	Hour	Summary of Events and Information	Remarks and references to Appendices
BEAUCOURT	25/7/18	2 p.m.	58th Divn Op. Order 131 received; detailed instructions for alterations in Divsl. Boundary.	
	29/7/18	noon	58th Divn. Warning Order received, reference relief of 58 Divn. by 12th Divn. August 2–4th 1918.	
	30/7/18	8am	58th Divn. O.O. 132 received. 175 Inf Bde relieves 174 Inf. Bde. night July 30–31st 1918.	
		2 pm	Preliminary handing-over arrangements discussed with Signals 12th Divn.	
	31/7/18	1am	Oper Order 133 received from Divsl H.Q. ordering extension of 173rd Inf Bde front.	

[signature] Major H.Q.
O.C. 58th DIVISIONAL SIGNAL CO. R.E.

D. D. & L., London, E.C.
(A10266) Wt W5300/P713 750,000 2/18 Sch. 52 Forms/C2118/16.

58th Divl. Engineers

58th DIVISIONAL SIGNAL COMPANY

ROYAL ENGINEERS

A U G U S T   1 9 1 8

29

D.A.G.,
3rd Echelon

This war diary refers to 58th Divsl. Signal Company.

When forwarded, it was enclosed in an envelope showing unit to which it referred.

[signature]

25/9/18.

Lieut.Colonel,
A.A.& Q.M.G., 58th Division.

SECRET

H.Q.,
58th. Division.

Can you say from what Unit the attached War Diary originated please.

G.H.Q.,
3rd. Echelon.
22nd September, 1918.

[signature] Yates
Major,
D.A.A.G.,
for D.A.G.

Instructions regarding War Diaries and Intelligence Summaries are contained in F. S. Regs., Part II. and the Staff Manual respectively. Title pages will be prepared in manuscript.

WAR DIARY
or
INTELLIGENCE SUMMARY.
(Erase heading not required.)

58 D Signals

Army Form C. 2118.

VIII 20

Place	Date	Hour	Summary of Events and Information	Remarks and references to Appendices
BEAUCOURT	1/8/18	2am	58th Divn. Operation Order 134 received; Division being relieved by 12th Divn. 10am August 4/18. Move to VIGNACOURT.	
	2/8/18	3pm	Destination of Divnl. H.Q. on relief altered to QUERRIEU	
	3/8/18	2pm	Transport leave BEAUCOURT for QUERRIEU.	
		6pm	58th Div. Op. Or. 135 received, ordering moves of 173 and 174 Inf Bdes. to new Area.	
	4/8/18	8am	58th Divn Op. Or. 136 received cancelling No 135, and amending moves of 173 and 174 Bdes.	
	4/8/18	10am	Closed at BEAUCOURT and reopened at QUERRIEU same hour	
QUERRIEU	4/8/18	6pm	58th Div Op. Or. 137 received. 174 Bde Gp. to take over from 18th Divn. portion of Corps front on night Aug. 5-6th	
	6/8/18	2am	58th Divn Op. Or. 138 received, move of 173 Bde to Valley J28a and c.	
	7/8/18	2pm	O.O. 139 received from 58th Divn. Scheme of proposed attack by the Divn. Date and hour to be notified.	

D. D. & L., London, E.C.
(A10266) Wt W5300/P713 750,000 2/18 Sch. 52 Forms/C2118/16.

Army Form C. 2118.

Instructions regarding War Diaries and Intelligence Summaries are contained in F. S. Regs., Part II. and the Staff Manual respectively. Title pages will be prepared in manuscript.

WAR DIARY
or
INTELLIGENCE SUMMARY.
(Erase heading not required.)

Place	Date	Hour	Summary of Events and Information	Remarks and references to Appendices
QUERRIEU	7/8/18	6 pm	Opened Advanced Signal Office at J.19.c.3.5	
J.19.c.3.5.	8/8/18	5.40 am	Zero hour for attack.	
	9/8/18.	1 am	58th Div O.O. 140 received – scheme for continuation of attack	
	9/8/18.	6 am	—"— —"— 141 further to above.	
	9/8/18	2 pm	—"— —"— 142 amplifying & amending instructions in 141.	
	11/8/18	5.30 pm	Zero hour – second phase of attack	
	12/8/18	noon	58th Div Op. Or. 143 received – relief of 175 Inf. Bde. night Aug 12–13th and proposed move of Division.	
		3.30 pm	Op. Or. 144 received. Further instruction re Divl. move to ST. GRATIEN.	
		5.30 pm	" " 145 " Brigade moves.	
	13/8/18.	10 am	Closed at J.19.c.3.5. and reopened at ST. GRATIEN same hour.	
ST. GRATIEN	14/8/18		Training programme arranged – to include visual training and station work	

D. D. & L., London, E.C.
(A10266) Wt W5300/P713 750,000 2/18 Sch. 52 Forms/C2118/16.

Instructions regarding War Diaries and Intelligence Summaries are contained in F. S. Regs., Part II, and the Staff Manual respectively. Title pages will be prepared in manuscript.

WAR DIARY
or
INTELLIGENCE SUMMARY.
(*Erase heading not required.*)

Army Form C. 2118.

Place	Date	Hour	Summary of Events and Information	Remarks and references to Appendices
			work	
ST GRATIEN	14/8/18		for operators and signallers, and general morning parade daily for musketry drill, gas instruction, squad + company drill etc.	
	20/8/18	6pm	58th Divn G/S 3455 recd. 174 Inf Bde at disposal of 18th Divn from mdnt. 20/21st Aug.	
	21/8/18	3pm	58th Divn. Op. Order 146 received. 58th Divn in Corps reserve for Corps attack. Moves of 174 and 175 Bdes specified.	
	22/8/18	4.45am	Zero hour for Corps attack.	
	22/8/18	2.25am	174 Inf. Bde. opened at HEILLY and closed at FRECHENCOURT	
	22/8/18	6.30am	175 Inf Bde opened at J19d55 and closed at FRECHENCOURT	
	23/8/18	9/15am	174 Inf Bde passes to 18th Div + opens HQ at J21b5.4 with 54 Inf Bde. 175 Inf Bde comes under Command of 47 DIV	
		9/30am	173 Inf Bde moves to HEILLY HALT	
		8.45pm	173 Inf Bde moves to K14b22	

D. D. & L., London, E.C.
(A10266) Wt W5300/P713 750,000 2/18 Sch. 52 Forms/C2118/16.

Army Form C. 2118.

Instructions regarding War Diaries and Intelligence Summaries are contained in F. S. Regs., Part II. and the Staff Manual respectively. Title pages will be prepared in manuscript.

WAR DIARY
or
INTELLIGENCE SUMMARY.
(Erase heading not required.)

Place	Date	Hour	Summary of Events and Information	Remarks and references to Appendices
ST GRATIEN	23/8/18	10.15pm	58 Div ordered to relieve 47 Div at 10am 24th	
	24/8/18	10am	58 Div opened at HEILLY and closed at St GRATIEN. with 175 and 140 Inf Bdes in Line - Hqrs L1b22. 173 + 142 Bdes at K17a8.3.	
		2.45p	O.O. 140 received. 174 Inf Bde returns to 58 Div	
	25/8/18	6.30am	Adv Div Hq opened at K14b22 S. of MORLANCOURT.	
		12.30pm	Div Hq opens at K14b22. 140 141 142 Inf Bdes return to 47 Div. 173 Inf Bde relieve 140 Bde 174 Bde relieve 175 Inf Bde	
	26/8/18	4.55am	173 + 174 Inf Bdes attack 4.55am.	
		11am	175 Inf Bde moves forward to position of readiness establishing Hq at B28d25.	
	27/8/18	4.55am	173 + 174 Inf Bdes attack.	
	28/8/18	3pm	Div Hq closes K14b22 reopening same hour L1b22.	
		mn	173 + 174 Bdes relieved by 175 Inf Bde Hqrs A19b41.	
	29/8/18	6pm	175 Inf Bde moves to Y Wood A23b22.	
	30/8/18	6am	175 Inf Bde moves to B26d59 HINDLEG WOOD.	
		3pm	Div Hq closes ~~W~~ L1b22 reopening A19b41 same hour.	
	31/8/18	4am	174th Bde relieves 175 Inf Bde and opens Hqrs at B26d59	

D. D. & L., London, E.C.
(A10266) Wt.W5300/P713 750,000 2/18 Sch. 52 Forms/C2118/16.

14

Instructions regarding War Diaries and Intelligence Summaries are contained in F. S. Regs., Part II. and the Staff Manual respectively. Title pages will be prepared in manuscript.

September 1918.

WAR DIARY
or
INTELLIGENCE SUMMARY.
(*Erase heading not required.*)

58 D Signals

Army Form C. 2118.

VII 21

Place	Date	Hour	Summary of Events and Information	Remarks and references to Appendices
Parcount A 196 5-2	1st		Division attacks 5.30 am with 173 Bde.	
			Communications established with 3 Bdes of 74th Division. Traffic heavy.	
		11.50pm	Command of sector passes to GOC 74th Div. Change over of Communication takes 2 hours owing to lines being cut by heavy bombing. Div HQs remains in the same place.	
	2nd		Day spent in overhauling & checking equipment.	
	3rd		All available men are employed salving cable 12½ miles of D8 twisted recovered mostly from lines laid out by this unit.	
			Two men per battalion report for PBA Course.	
	4th		Salving of cable continues. 4½ miles recovered. PBA Course commences.	
			Visit to Divisional Signal School at HEILLY.	
	5th		Salving of cable continues 3½ miles recovered. Attend Conference with Wireless Officer at Corps HQs to discuss the question of "abolition or retention of loop sets".	

D. D. & L., London, E.C.
(A10266) Wt W5300/P713 750,000 2/18 Sch. 52 Forms/C2118/16.

Army Form C. 2118.

Instructions regarding War Diaries and Intelligence Summaries are contained in F. S. Regs., Part II. and the Staff Manual respectively. Title pages will be prepared in manuscript.

WAR DIARY
or
INTELLIGENCE SUMMARY.
(Erase heading not required.)

Place	Date	Hour	Summary of Events and Information	Remarks and references to Appendices
			It was generally agreed that "loop sets should be retained & if necessary PBA's abolished"	
	6th		Information received from G. that 58th Div would relieve 47th Div with HQs at BOUCHAVESNES at 8am next day. Visit with 2/Command to 47th rear at MAUREPAS and advanced at BOUCHAVESNES. On return Cable Section with a lorry of stores & personnel sent forward.	
BOUCHAVESNES C 20 b 3.1	7th	8am	Office opens. Lines to forward brigades dis. Detachments sent out to relay lines forward & to complete certain lines to metallic.	
		12.10pm	All lines forward working satisfactorily with more superimposed.	
			Reconnoitre for suitable advanced HQs & G informed	
GURLU WOOD D 22 a 2 4	8th	2.30pm	New office established. Lines to forward brigades working well. Wireless communication also established & sets working well with R9 signals.	

D. D. & L., London, E.C.
(A10266) Wt W5300/P713 750,000 2/18 Sch. 52 Forms/C2118/16.

Instructions regarding War Diaries and Intelligence Summaries are contained in F. S. Regs., Part II. and the Staff Manual respectively. Title pages will be prepared in manuscript.

WAR DIARY
or
INTELLIGENCE SUMMARY.
(Erase heading not required.)

Army Form C. 2118.

Place	Date	Hour	Summary of Events and Information	Remarks and references to Appendices
	9th		Existing lines improved & certain administrative services connected to exchange.	
			A forward exchange installed at LIERAMONT. All forward lines pass thro this office. Existing routes rewired & made use of.	
	10th		Reconnaissance for buried routes. Shallow bury found in vicinity of Lieramont.	
			Route diagram of communication attached marked "A".	"A".
			Message & DRLS heavy as follows:-	
			Messages - 761 - DRLS. - 342 -	
	11th		Shallow bury repaired & working in final scheme of communications to brigades. Further buries reconnoitred.	
	12th		New auxiliary 4pr poled cable route started from HQrs to forward exchange at LIERAMONT. Light hop poles & D8 cable used. Bays each 40 yds. Strength of party 1 officer & 12 ORs (excluding drivers for wagons.) Heavy rain renders construction slow.	

D. D. & L., London, E.C.
(A10266) Wt W5300/P713 750,000 2/18 Sch. 52 Forms/C2118/16.

Army Form C. 2118.

Instructions regarding War Diaries and Intelligence Summaries are contained in F. S. Regs., Part II. and the Staff Manual respectively. Title pages will be prepared in manuscript.

WAR DIARY
or
INTELLIGENCE SUMMARY.
(Erase heading not required.)

Place	Date	Hour	Summary of Events and Information	Remarks and references to Appendices
	13th		Poled route to Lieramont completed	
	14th		Leading in to advanced office in Lieramont completed. 2 reinforcements arrive. One man states "Transferred from ROD & trained for 2 months at Abbeville, trade F.L.D." On proficient rate of pay on transfer.	
	15th		Advanced exchange position taken over by Sigs 18th Div. Party sent forward to construct suitable dug out for exchange.	
	16th		Exchange installed in new position. All lines now clear of village of Lieramont which is periodically shelled. Certain routes in the area forward of Lieramont poled to avoid tank traffic.	
	17th		Final preparation for Z day. During night tank traffic brings down poled route. One Sig A. reinforcement arrives. Trained in accordance with S.S.T.C syllabus for Sig A.	

D. D. & L., London, E.C.
(A10266) Wt W5300/P713 750,000 2/18 Sch. 52 Forms/C2118/16.

WAR DIARY
or
INTELLIGENCE SUMMARY.
(Erase heading not required.)

Army Form C. 2118.

Instructions regarding War Diaries and Intelligence Summaries are contained in F. S. Regs., Part II. and the Staff Manual respectively. Title pages will be prepared in manuscript.

Place	Date	Hour	Summary of Events and Information	Remarks and references to Appendices
			The lead cable buried in vicinity of Lieramont cut in 3 places by men of a reserve battalion digging shelters. Buried route was not marked.	
	18th	5.20am	Zero hour. All communication working satisfactorily. No disturbance during night from hostile fire or bombs. An advance to final object of 2500x was made. W.T. officer installed a trench set also a forward & rear loop set east of "old no man's land". Working to & from trench set unsatisfactory owing to severe jamming. Loop sets worked well. Visual & pigeons also used but no new lessons learnt. W.T. Officer with 3 operators caught 6 prisoners who had escaped the notice of the mopping up party.	
			Traffic during the day heavy. Messages dealt with 829.	

D. D. & L., London, E.C.
(A10266) Wt W5300/P713 750,000 2/18 Sch. 52 Forms/C2118/16.

Instructions regarding War Diaries and Intelligence Summaries are contained in F. S. Regs., Part II. and the Staff Manual respectively. Title pages will be prepared in manuscript.

WAR DIARY
or
INTELLIGENCE SUMMARY.
(Erase heading not required.)

Army Form C. 2118.

Place	Date	Hour	Summary of Events and Information	Remarks and references to Appendices
	19th		Brigade relief. No event of importance	
	20th		Lt Smallwood No 5 Section awarded Military Cross.	
			New poled route from LIERAMONT to Quarry commenced	
			Forward Exchange move to Quarry and advance of	
			1500x. Comparatively little work involved owing to	
			move taking place along main line of communications	
			Spr W.S Cormack awarded Military Medal	
	21		No event of importance	
	22		No event of importance	
	23		Orders for relief of division issued. Cable Section	
			sent to CATERPILLAR VALLEY to prepare new HQrs.	
	24		Office closes at 11 am & reopens CATERPILLAR VALLEY	
			at same hour. Attached letter marked B issued by	B
			Q to units concerned on 22nd.	
	25		In communication with 3 Infy Bdes. Orders for division	
			to move to new Area received.	

D. D. & L., London, E.C.
(A10266) Wt W5300/P713 750,000 2/18 Sch. 52 Forms/C2118/16.

Instructions regarding War Diaries and Intelligence Summaries are contained in F. S. Regs., Part II. and the Staff Manual respectively. Title pages will be prepared in manuscript.

WAR DIARY
or
INTELLIGENCE SUMMARY.
(Erase heading not required.)

Army Form C. 2118.

Place	Date	Hour	Summary of Events and Information	Remarks and references to Appendices
	26		Company moves to Entraining station at HEILLY. Two lorries with stores etc leave for new area with sufficient personnel and instruments to open up new office	
Villers Chatel	27		Company arrives 2.15 pm – Train 11 hours overdue on 6 hrs journey.	
	28.		Advance party send forward to 24th Div. to get into touch with situation	
	29.		Further personnel and stores sent forward	
Sains-en Gohelle	30		Company moves at 8.15 am to new hqrs. Office opens at 4 pm at which hour GOC 58th Div assumes command of sector. Box car breaks down & towed to MT Coy. Trouble unknown.	

C. Firth Major
OC 58th Signal Coy RE.
30-9-18.

D. D. & L., London, E.C.
(A10266) Wt W5300/P713 750,000 2/18 Sch. 52 Forms/C2118/16.

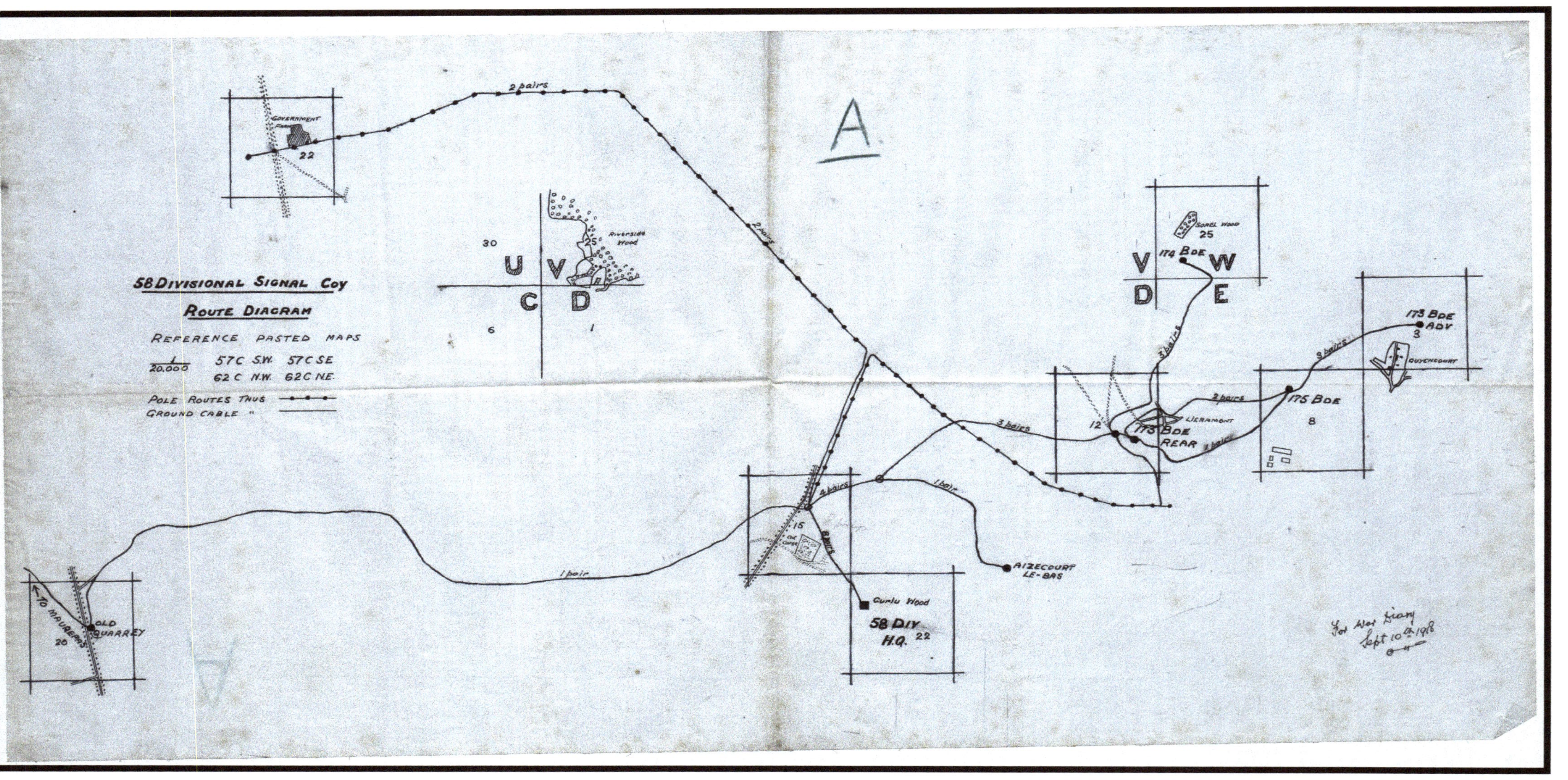
A
58 Divisional Signal Coy
Route Diagram
Reference pasted maps
1/20,000 57C S.W. 57C S.E
62 C N.W. 62C N.E.
Pole Routes thus
Ground Cable "
2 pairs
Government
22
30
U V
C D
6
1
25
Riverside Wood
Sorel Wood
25
174 Bde
V W
D E
173 Bde
Adv.
3
Guyencourt
3 pairs
2 pairs
175 Bde
8
12
173 Bde
Rear
Lieramont
1 pair
4 pairs
15
8 pairs
Aizecourt
Le-Bas
Gurlu Wood
58 Div
H.Q. 22
To Maurepas
Old Quarrey
20
For War Diary
Sept 10th 1918

6 October 1918.

WAR DIARY
or
INTELLIGENCE SUMMARY.
(Erase heading not required.)

58 D Signals

Army Form C. 2118.

Instructions regarding War Diaries and Intelligence Summaries are contained in F. S. Regs., Part II. and the Staff Manual respectively. Title pages will be prepared in manuscript.

88 22

Place	Date	Hour	Summary of Events and Information	Remarks and references to Appendices
SAINS-EN-GOHELLE	1st		Information received that Enemy was commencing to withdraw. Arrangements made for Inf + Artillery brigades to move forward on buried routes.	
	2nd		174 + 173 Brigades move forward. Communication established as arranged. All power buzzers + amplifiers remained in their positions + did not move forward owing to lack of men for carrying. 173 bde rear at BULLY closes down + 174 bde rear taken over by [illegible] who man the office as an exchange only. Owing to 14 men being loaned to the 4 + 5 Area detachments.	
	3rd		Brigades move forward to new positions except 173 bde who are withdrawn to reserve. All buried lines to new positions very costly necessitating two pairs of D8 being laid. Buried lines too costly for more working. A.D. Signals informed.	

D. D. & L., London, E.C.
(A10266) Wt W5300/P713 750,000 2/18 Sch. 52 Forms/C2118/16.

Instructions regarding War Diaries and Intelligence Summaries are contained in F. S. Regs., Part II. and the Staff Manual respectively. Title pages will be prepared in manuscript.

WAR DIARY
or
INTELLIGENCE SUMMARY.
(Erase heading not required.)

Army Form C. 2118.

Place	Date	Hour	Summary of Events and Information	Remarks and references to Appendices
	4		First course for pigeoneers terminates & second course assembles. 19 men attend each course. New HQrs at Fosse 11 M & B central prepared for arrival of Div HQrs. Second in Command with a cable section sent forward to do the necessary work.	
	5.		Visit by D D Signals 1st Army. New HQrs and 173 Bde visited. Lack of visual commented upon. Such a scheme considered unnecessary owing to proximity of Bn HQrs to cable head. Visual used between Coy & battn. Shortage of cable explained but no prospect of a better supply.	
	6.		Visit to Signal School. Nothing of importance to report.	
	7.		Nothing of importance to report.	

D. D. & L., London, E.C.
(A10166) Wt W5300/P713 750,000 2/18 Sch. 52 Forms/C2118/16.

Army Form C. 2118.

Instructions regarding War Diaries and Intelligence Summaries are contained in F. S. Regs., Part II. and the Staff Manual respectively. Title pages will be prepared in manuscript.

WAR DIARY
or
INTELLIGENCE SUMMARY.
(*Erase heading not required.*)

Place	Date	Hour	Summary of Events and Information	Remarks and references to Appendices
	8		Nothing of importance to report	
	9.		Daimler Lorry & Wolseley Car to workshops for overhaul. 3 ton Lorry from M T Coy to replace Seven Berna Lorry undergoing repair.	
	10		Two officers & 52 OR join Signal School	
	11.		Nothing of importance to report.	
	12.		Order received that HQ's will move to FOSSE 11 & open at 1500.	
FOSSE 11.	13.		HQ's move to Fosse 11. All lines to brigades working well.	
	14.		In order to facilitate communications with brigades & brigades with battalions paras 5 6 & 7 of attached letter marked "A" circulated to units. Every facility given by G with regard to Brigade HQ's.	"A"

D. D. & L., London, E.C.
(A10266) Wt W5300/P713 750,000 2/18 Sch. 52 Forms/C2118/16.

Instructions regarding War Diaries and Intelligence Summaries are contained in F. S. Regs., Part II. and the Staff Manual respectively. Title pages will be prepared in manuscript.

WAR DIARY
or
INTELLIGENCE SUMMARY.
(Erase heading not required.)

Army Form C. 2118.

Place	Date	Hour	Summary of Events and Information	Remarks and references to Appendices
	15		Visit by DD Sigs 5th Army on transfer from 1st to 5th Army. Brigade HQs of 173 & 174 move to HARNES.	
	16.		Two officers proceed to prepare new HQ at MONTIGNY.	
MONTIGNY	17.		HQs move to MONTIGNY and open at noon – Difficulty experienced in getting transport – lorries in particular through LENS. Brigades move forward COURRIERES and OIGNIES. Owing to rapidity of advance efforts concentrated on ~~of~~ maintaining one metallic forward to serve 3 brigades. Rear brigade double transformer to forward brigade with centre brigade intermediate. W.T. truck set moves with forward brigade to ~~faker~~ facilitate disposal of messages	
	18.		Brigades move OIGNIES and OSTRICOURT and line	

D. D. & L., London, E.C. (A10266) Wt W5300/P713 750,000 2/18 Sch. 52 Forms/C2118/16.

Instructions regarding War Diaries and Intelligence Summaries are contained in F. S. Regs., Part II. and the Staff Manual respectively. Title pages will be prepared in manuscript.

WAR DIARY
or
INTELLIGENCE SUMMARY.
(Erase heading not required.)

Army Form C. 2118.

Place	Date	Hour	Summary of Events and Information	Remarks and references to Appendices
			extended by cable wagon. During night morse + telephone working well. Two offrs proceed forward to open up new office at MONCHEAUX.	
MONCHEAUX	19		HQ's open MONCHEAUX noon. Attached marked "B" moved.	"B"
BERSEE			HQ open BERSEE 3 pm. Change of HQ due to rapid move of advance guards. Through to 3 brigades by morse and telephone	
	20		Owing to brigades move during the day the following system was commenced. An officer with cable section, WT station, + 3 office telegraphists proceed 6.30 am + follow the advance guard with cable train. Section halt and open office at a village notified to all concerned the night before. This office remains open + receives messages for transmission	

D. D. & L., London, E.C.
(A10266) Wt W5300/P713 750,000 2/18 Sch. 52 Forms/C2118/16.

Instructions regarding War Diaries and Intelligence Summaries are contained in F. S. Regs., Part II. and the Staff Manual respectively. Title pages will be prepared in manuscript.

WAR DIARY
or
INTELLIGENCE SUMMARY.
(Erase heading not required.)

Army Form C. 2118.

Place	Date	Hour	Summary of Events and Information	Remarks and references to Appendices
			until brigades are through from the night HQ's. The dropped office then closes and joins one or other of the leading brigades. The same procedure is adopted the following day. Communication to Corps along lateral to 15 Div who dispose.	
MOUCHIN	21		HQ move to MOUCHIN at 2 pm. No communication with three brigades. Communication to Corps along our forward line of 20th via NOMAIN - BERSEE and MONCHEAUX. This method unsatisfactory as an office has to be installed at NOMAIN to transmit, due to length of line. Further detachment detailed for reeling up unable to proceed with work & reduces stock of cable. Each day the Artillery brigade covering the inf bde obtains communication with CRA thro' Inf bde exchange.	

D. D. & L., London, E.C.
(A10266) Wt W5300/P713 750,000 2/18 Sch. 52 Forms/C2118/16.

Instructions regarding War Diaries and Intelligence Summaries are contained in F. S. Regs., Part II. and the Staff Manual respectively. Title pages will be prepared in manuscript.

WAR DIARY
or
INTELLIGENCE SUMMARY.
(Erase heading not required.)

Army Form C. 2118.

Place	Date	Hour	Summary of Events and Information	Remarks and references to Appendices
	22		Permanent lines left by enemy reconnoitred.	
	23.		Enemy permanent route MOUCHIN - RUMIGIES - RONGY found good except at 2 places where poles have been cut. Gaps bridged with cable & 2 prs put through to RONGY for use to 175 Bde & artillery bde.	
			HQ 173 bde move from RONGY to HOWARDRIES. Owing to lack of accomodation J cable section returns to MOUCHIN. Swin Burna lorry returns from H T Coy	
	24		a general straighten up. Line to rt flank div through & working	
	25.		Enemy permanent route made good - New poles and 60lb GI used	
			Electric light set transferred from GS wagon to Daimler lorry.	
			Left flank div move to LAGRANERIE. Lateral communication established	

D. D. & L., London, E.C. (A10266) Wt W5300/P713 750,000 2/18 Sch. 52 Forms/C2118/16.

Instructions regarding War Diaries and Intelligence Summaries are contained in F. S. Regs., Part II. and the Staff Manual respectively. Title pages will be prepared in manuscript.

WAR DIARY
or
INTELLIGENCE SUMMARY.
(Erase heading not required.)

Army Form C. 2118.

Place	Date	Hour	Summary of Events and Information	Remarks and references to Appendices
	26		Party again work on Permanent Route. All locals straightened up.	
			174 Bde move to QUESNOY	
	27.		Nothing of importance to report.	
	28		Lt HAYNES MC assumes duty as W/T officer vice 2Lt HOLMES wounded & to England. Divisional sector very quiet.	
	29. 30 31	}	Nothing of importance to report	
			31-10-18. [illegible] Major OC. 58th Signal Coy RE	

D. D. & L., London, E.C.
(A10266) Wt W5300/P713 750,000 2/18 Sch. 52 Forms/C2118/16.

C O P Y -

CONFIDENTIAL.

G.S. 3550

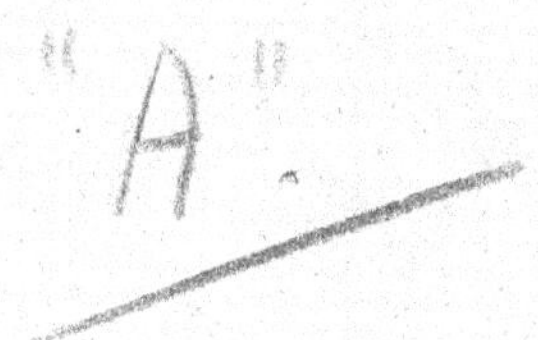

173rd. Inf. Brigade
174th. Inf. Brigade
175th. Inf. Brigade

1. The Divisional Commander has formed the opinion that our advance has been too slow, and that the enemy rear-guards are not being pressed as closely as they should be. This he attributes largely to Commanders not keeping in sufficiently close touch with operations.

2. Although the present conditions are not exactly those contemplated in Field Service Regulations, when the Commander of an advance guard normally moves at the head of the main guard, yet they more closely resemble those conditions than trench warfare, in which Brigade, Battalion and even Company Commanders live in dugouts at a considerable distance in rear of their commands.

3. The Divisional Commander lays down that in future, as a general rule, Brigade Commanders should establish their Headquarters at least as far forward as the position of their reserve Battalion, and that Battalion Commanders should similarly be at least as far forward as their support Companies.

4. Since the conditions are more trying than in trench warfare owing to the constant movement, and the difficulties in getting up rations, Battalions should not be kept in the Front Line for more than 48 hours if it can be avoided. Brigade frontages and reliefs, will, if possible be so arranged that either Brigades will only be required to remain in the Front line for a short time or else shall only be required to keep one battalion in front line.

5. The difficulties of communication must be expected to increase as the advance continues, and full use will be made of visual signalling, pigeons and wireless, in order to economise cable wherever possible.

6. It is the duty of the H.Q. Section of the Divisional Signal Company to keep open communications between Division and Brigade Headquarters, but in order that it may be possible for them to do so with the limited material available it will usually be necessary for Divisional Headquarters to lay down the line on which Brigade Headquarters are to be established, although the wishes of Brigade Commanders will be considered as far as possible.

7. When two Brigades are in the line it will often be necessary that the Headquarters of both shall be together near the centre of the Divisional Area.

(Signed) A. M. Davis,
Lieut-Col.
General Staff, 58th. (London) Division.

13th. October 1918.

C O P Y -

CONFIDENTIAL.

G.S. 3550

173rd. Inf. Brigade
174th. Inf. Brigade
175th. Inf. Brigade

1. The Divisional Commander has formed the opinion that our advance has been too slow, and that the enemy rear-guards are not being pressed as closely as they should be. This he attributes largely to Commanders not keeping in sufficiently close touch with operations.

2. Although the present conditions are not exactly those contemplated in Field Service Regulations, when the Commander of an advance guard normally moves at the head of the main guard, yet they more closely resemble those conditions than trench warfare, in which Brigade, Battalion and even Company Commanders live in dugouts at a considerable distance in rear of their commands.

3. The Divisional Commander lays down that in future, as a general rule, Brigade Commanders should establish their Headquarters at least as far forward as the position of their reserve Battalion, and that Battalion Commanders should similarly be at least as far forward as their support Companies.

4. Since the conditions are more trying than in trench warfare owing to the constant movement, and the difficulties in getting up rations, Battalions should not be kept in the Front Line for more than 48 hours if it can be avoided. Brigade frontages and reliefs, will, if possible be so arranged that either Brigades will only be required to remain in the Front line for a short time or else shall only be required to keep one battalion in front line.

5. The difficulties of communication must be expected to increase as the advance continues, and full use will be made of visual signalling, pigeons and wireless, in order to economise cable wherever possible.

6. It is the duty of the H.Q. Section of the Divisional Signal Company to keep open communications between Division and Brigade Headquarters, but in order that it may be possible for them to do so with the limited material available it will usually be necessary for Divisional Headquarters to lay down the line on which Brigade Headquarters are to be established, although the wishes of Brigade Commanders will be considered as far as possible.

7. When two Brigades are in the line it will often be necessary that the Headquarters of both shall be together near the centre of the Divisional Area.

(Signed) A. N. Davis,
Lieut-Col.
General Staff, 58th. (London) Division.

13th. October 1918.

- COPY -

"B"

Keep for War Diary

58th (LONDON) DIVISION.

58th Dibn.
G.S. 8/159.

Owing to difficulties of telephonic communications conversations between Brigades and Divisions must be limited as far as possible.

Priority of calls will be allotted as follows:-

G.O.C.
"G".
"Q".
C.R.A.
C.R.E.
58th Bn, M.G.C.
A.D.M.S.
D.A.D.O.S.

Conversations must be restricted as far as possible. Should any branch have an important call to put through for which they are unable to obtain use of the line application should be made to "G" Office.

C M Davis
Lieut-Colonel,
General Staff, 58th (London) Division.

19th October, 1918.

Distribution.

A.D.C. for G.O.C.
C.R.A.
C.R.E.
173rd Inf. Brigade.
174th Inf. Brigade.
175th Inf. Brigade.
58th Bn. M.G.Corps.
Signals.
A.D.M.S.
D.A.D.O.S.
"Q".

4

Instructions regarding War Diaries and Intelligence Summaries are contained in F. S. Regs., Part II. and the Staff Manual respectively. Title pages will be prepared in manuscript.

WAR DIARY
or
INTELLIGENCE SUMMARY.
(Erase heading not required.)

58 Div Sig Co RE
Vol 23

Army Form C. 2118.

Place	Date	Hour	Summary of Events and Information	Remarks and references to Appendices
MOUCHIN	Nov 1st. 1918	10am	173rd Inf. Bde moves to NOMAIN.	W.H.J.
	3/11/18		Maj. W.E. GURRY M.C. R.E. takes over command of the Company, vice Maj. C.W.M. FIRTH M.C. (DORSETS) appointed A.D. Signals XXII Corps.	W.H.J.
	5/11/18		Preliminary reconnaissance made for cable routes required for proposed attempt to force crossing of SCHELDT.	W.H.J.
	8/11/18		Enemy retiring – Adv. Div office opened at RONGY Chau. temporarily and moved on to BLEHARIES at 4 pm. 174 Bde ordered to LAPLAIGNE but lack of Bridges renders this impossible & Hqrs opened at BLEHARIES with Adv. Bde at LAPLAIGNE.	W.H.J.
BLEHARIES	9/11/18		173 Bde moves to RONGY. Div Hqrs closes MOUCHIN 1200 hrs reopening BLEHARIES same hour. 174 Bde on Left 175 Bde on Right continue advance. Adv Div Office opened ROUILLON 11:30 hrs. 175 Bde opens HQ at WIERS 1500 hrs 174 Bde at BRASMENIL.	W.H.J.
WIERS	10/11/18		No lorry transport possible as no lorry bridges existing. D.H.Q. opens WIERS 1400 hrs. 173 Bde to BLEHARIES. 174 to BASECLES 175 to ECACHERIES.	W.H.J.
BELOEIL	11/11/18		Div Hq to BASECLES 1100 hrs and on to BELOEIL Chau 1600 hrs. Hostilities cease 1100 hrs.	

D. D. & L., London, E.C.
(A10266) Wt W5300/P713 750,000 2/18 Sch. 52 Forms/C2118/16.

Instructions regarding War Diaries and Intelligence Summaries are contained in F. S. Regs., Part II. and the Staff Manual respectively. Title pages will be prepared in manuscript.

WAR DIARY
or
INTELLIGENCE SUMMARY.
(Erase heading not required.)

Army Form C. 2118.

Place	Date	Hour	Summary of Events and Information	Remarks and references to Appendices
BELOEIL	11/11/18		173 Bde moves to BASECLES 174 at GROSAGE moving later to VAUDIGNIES 175 Bde at ECACHERIES Lorries reach BELOEIL 1700 hrs having travelled via ANTOING TOURNAI and LEUZE.	
	12/11/18		175 Bde move to STAMBRUGES.	
	18/11/18		174 Bde move to PERUWELZ.	
	19/11/18		First Examination of Candidates for instruction by Signal Coy in accordance with Divnl Education Scheme. MG Bn to ROUCOURT	
	20/11/18		Examinations Continue.	
	21/11/18		Div HQ closes BELOEIL opens PERUWELZ 1200 hrs.	
	25/11/18		Classes for Instruction in Telegraphy Wireless + Adv Electricity + Magnetism assemble	
	28/11/18		Lt T.O BALK to England on 3 weeks Course at Oxford under Education Scheme	

B. Watson Capt R.E.
For O.C. 58th DIVISIONAL SIGNAL CO. R.E.

D. D. & L., London, E.C.
(A10266) Wt W5300/P713 750,000 2/18 Sch. 52 Forms/C2118/16.

7

Instructions regarding War Diaries and Intelligence Summaries are contained in F. S. Regs., Part II. and the Staff Manual respectively. Title pages will be prepared in manuscript.

WAR DIARY
or
INTELLIGENCE SUMMARY.

(Erase heading not required.)

Army Form C. 2118.

58 D. Signal Coy

Vol 24

Place	Date	Hour	Summary of Events and Information	Remarks and references to Appendices
PERUWELZ	1/12/18 to 31/12/18		The Educational Classes which began last month continue. Lectures in French and extra lectures on Magnetism and Electricity were introduced early in the current month. Arrangements were made for lectures on the Geography of the British Isles to be given for the benefit of men desirous of taking City & Guilds Examinations. These lectures will commence with the New Year.	
			Two Association Football teams (A + B) were raised from Hqrs & No 1 Section of the Company and two more (C + D) from the men attached for Educational training. C Team however dropped out. A Divisional Hqrs League was formed consisting of 3 Signal teams, Div Employment Coy, Hqrs M.G. Battn & Div Hqrs. The following matches were played. Dec 3. Sigs D v Sigs B result 2 goals – 1 goal	
			7 Sigs A v Employment Co. " 2 – 1 "	
			Sigs D v M.G. Bn " 1 " – 2 "	
			9. Sigs B v 3/7th Transport 1 " – 3 "	
			14 Sigs D v Sigs A. 4 " – 0	
			15 Sigs B v RA Hqrs 7 " – 1	
			19 Sigs A v Sigs B. 1 – 0	
			18. Sigs D v Employment Co. 0 – 0	
			21 Sigs A v RA Hqrs 5 " – 1 "	
			30 Sigs D v 3/7th Transport 2 – 2	

D. D. & L., London, E.C.
(A10266) Wt W5300/P713 750,000 2/18 Sch. 52 Forms/C2118/16.

Instructions regarding War Diaries and Intelligence Summaries are contained in F. S. Regs., Part II. and the Staff Manual respectively. Title pages will be prepared in manuscript.

WAR DIARY
or
INTELLIGENCE SUMMARY.
(Erase heading not required.)

Army Form C. 2118.

Place	Date	Hour	Summary of Events and Information	Remarks and references to Appendices
PERUWELZ.	1/12/18 to 24/12/18		Besides these league games various friendly matches were played within the Company. A Rugby XV was got up from Div. Tps the nucleus of which was found from the Company but owing to bad weather only two matches were played one against the M.G. Battn & one against the 7th Battn both resulting in a victory.	
	DEC 25th		Christmas Day. The Christmas Dinner for the men was held at midday in the Central Mess Room (in the Monastery) which was very successfully decorated for the occasion under the supervision of the CSM. The Divisional Commander and Col. Davies GSO1. came in during the Dinner. The General made a brief speech which was greeted with three cheers & "For He's a jolly good fellow". The NCOs & Motor Cyclists had their Dinner in the evening.	
	26/12/18 to 31/12/18		Resumed normal activities. There is nothing of interest to record except that a Company dance was held on New Year's Eve in the Schoolroom next the Convent Peruwelz	

D. D. & L., London, E.C.
(A10266) Wt W5300/P713 750,000 2/18 Sch. 52 Forms/C2118/16.

Army Form C. 2118.

WAR DIARY
or
INTELLIGENCE SUMMARY.
(Erase heading not required.)

Instructions regarding War Diaries and Intelligence Summaries are contained in F. S. Regs., Part II. and the Staff Manual respectively. Title pages will be prepared in manuscript.

Place	Date	Hour	Summary of Events and Information	Remarks and references to Appendices
PERUWELZ.	31/12/18		Demobilisation By this date the principle of demobilisation by individuals and not by units had been laid down and from time to time instructions had been issued for the release of Coalminers, "Pivotal" men, Demobilisers, Guarantee Letter men, Long Service men & those both offices of posts etc where they would be trained for their subsequent careers. The War Office had issued orders that men on leave if in possession of a Guarantee Letter from a pre-war Employer need not return to duty. By the end of the month a demobilisation allotment of 27 men of these special categories per day had been received by the Division.	[illegible]

B. L. Clarkson
Capt. R.E. for
O.C. 56th DIVISIONAL SIGNAL CO. R.E.

D. D. & L., London, E.C.
(A10266) Wt W5300/P713 750,000 2/18 Sch. 52 Forms/C2118/16.

7 58

58 D Signals

VIII 25

Army Form C. 2118.

Instructions regarding War Diaries and Intelligence Summaries are contained in F. S. Regs., Part II. and the Staff Manual respectively. Title pages will be prepared in manuscript.

WAR DIARY
or
INTELLIGENCE SUMMARY.

(Erase heading not required.)

Place	Date	Hour	Summary of Events and Information	Remarks and references to Appendices
Peruwelz	1-31/1/19		Education The various educational classes have been continued, but owing to demobilisation, the numbers at the school had dwindled to 75 on the 31st. A class in Electricity, Magnetism & Telegraphy has been held each morning for the Tel[illegible] operators & a limited number of infantrymen who are P.O. servants, & prepare to sit the City & Guilds Examination in these subjects. The Sounder classes have been carried on each morning with tests in Sounder sending & receiving. The men attending these classes have had evening lectures in Electricity & Magnetism, & Telegraphy. On Jan 2nd 7th classes were started in Arithmetic & English for 16 O.Rs who wish to sit for the 2nd Class army certificate. The Wireless class has made satisfactory progress throughout the month.	

D. D. & L., London, E.C.
(A10266) Wt W5300/P713 750,000 2/18 Sch. 52 Forms/C2118/16.

Army Form C. 2118.

WAR DIARY
or
INTELLIGENCE SUMMARY.
(*Erase heading not required.*)

Instructions regarding War Diaries and Intelligence Summaries are contained in F. S. Regs., Part II. and the Staff Manual respectively. Title pages will be prepared in manuscript.

Place	Date	Hour	Summary of Events and Information	Remarks and references to Appendices
Perruwelz	1–31 Jan '19		On the 16th, the Corps Commander 1st Corps, inspected the school, & expressed himself as very pleased with what he saw. He made a short speech to the men which was much appreciated. Games have been as much as possible but owing to the snow & frosty weather since the 20th, it has not been possible to do much. On the 6th a very successful mounted paper chase was held. The following association matches have been played.	

Signals A	0 goal	V	2/7th Transport	1 goal
Signals	2 –	V	58th Div HQ	0 –
Signals B	0	V	173 Bn HQ	2 –
Signals	1	V	2/1 H C Fld Ambce	1
Signals	0	V	M.G. Bn	6
Signal office staff	0	V	D. Rs	1
Operators	1	V	Wireless	0
Signals	2	V	RAMC	5
"	1	V	8th London Regt	2

D. D. & L., London, E.C.
(A10266) Wt W5300/P713 750,000 2/18 Sch. 52 Forms/C2118/16.

Instructions regarding War Diaries and Intelligence Summaries are contained in F. S. Regs., Part II. and the Staff Manual respectively. Title pages will be prepared in manuscript.

WAR DIARY
or
INTELLIGENCE SUMMARY.
(Erase heading not required.)

Army Form C. 2118.

Place	Date	Hour	Summary of Events and Information	Remarks and references to Appendices
Pommereuil	1–31 Jan 19		It has not been possible to maintain a Rugby fifteen, but the Coy formed a combined team with H.Q. 173 Bde, & played two matches, both of which were won easily. During the month three successful dances were given by men of the Coy. to the local ladies who gave a return dance on the 27th. Otherwise there is nothing of interest to record. [illegible] Capt R.E. for O.C. 58th Div Sig Coy R.E.	

D. D. & L., London, E.C.
(A10266) Wt W5300/P713 750,000 2/18 Sch. 52 Forms/C2118/16.

58

Army Form C. 2118.

58th DIVISIONAL
SIGNAL Co. R.E.

14

WAR DIARY
or
INTELLIGENCE SUMMARY.
(Erase heading not required.)

Instructions regarding War Diaries and Intelligence Summaries are contained in F. S. Regs., Part II. and the Staff Manual respectively. Title pages will be prepared in manuscript.

Vol 26

Place	Date	Hour	Summary of Events and Information	Remarks and references to Appendices
Peruwelz	1-28/2/19.		Education The educational work was maintained in the Company, altho' the numbers of students slowly decreased through demobilization. Classes in telegraphy and general subjects were held as in the previous month. These continued until the 21st when orders were received to return to their units the few infantry signallers who were still under instruction. One small class for men of the Signal Company was held until the end of the month when the demobilization of signal personnel necessitated the closing of this class, as all available men were required for duty. The classes for men desirous of sitting for the City & Guilds Examinations in Electricity & Magnetism were closed as all students were demobilized. A class for men who wished to sit for the examination for the 2nd Class Army Certificate was formed at the beginning of the month. The examination was held on the 27th when four candidates sat from the Signal Company. Recreation Demobilization & a long spell of frost with some heavy falls of snow interfered very seriously with the sports programme: one friendly match (Association) was played between the Motor-Cyclists and the Signal Office Staff, the former winning by 2-0. Two successful dances at the Hôtel de Ville were given by the Company.	

T.O. Balk Lt R.W... R
OC 58 Div Sig Coy R.E.

D. D. & L., London, E.C.
(A10266) Wt W5300/P713 750,000 2/18 Sch. 52 Forms/C2118/16.

18 58

Instructions regarding War Diaries and Intelligence Summaries are contained in F. S. Regs., Part II. and the Staff Manual respectively. Title pages will be prepared in manuscript.

WAR DIARY
or
INTELLIGENCE SUMMARY.
(Erase heading not required.)

58th DIVISIONAL SIGNAL Co. R.E.

Army Form C. 2118.

Vol 27

Place	Date	Hour	Summary of Events and Information	Remarks and references to Appendices
Peruwelz	1-19/3/19		There is little of interest to report this month. On the 4th 58 Div Letter D 374 with instructions to reduce strength to Cadre A Establishment was received. The small numbers available for work after the reduction were employed in recovering cable as the units of the Division began to concentrate at Leuze.	
Leuze	19/3/19-31/3/19		Div Headquarters moved to Leuze. The Div Sig Office opened at Leuze at 1400 hrs on that date. The Signal Coy moved at the same time to Leuze, a small office being maintained at Peruwelz for the details who remained there. This office was closed 26/3/19.	

T.O. Balk Lt
OC 58 Div Sig Coy RE

D. D. & L., London, E.C.
(A10266) Wt W5300/P713 750,000 2/18 Sch. 52 Forms/C2118/16.

Instructions regarding War Diaries and Intelligence Summaries are contained in F. S. Regs., Part II. and the Staff Manual respectively. Title pages will be prepared in manuscript.

WAR DIARY
or
INTELLIGENCE SUMMARY.
(Erase heading not required.)

Army Form C. 2118.

58 D Sig Coy

Apl & May 19

28 & 29

58

Place	Date	Hour	Summary of Events and Information	Remarks and references to Appendices
Lunge	1/5/19 -31/5/19		1-31/5/19 30% of personnel demobilized in accordance with Mons Cadre 'A' Letter No D 12/192 of 11/4/19 No other events worthy of record occurred	
			T.O. Bath Lt OC 58 Div Sig Coy R.E.	

D. D. & L., London, E.C.
(A10266) Wt W5300/P713 750,000 2/18 Sch. 52 Forms/C2118/16.

Instructions regarding War Diaries and Intelligence Summaries are contained in F. S. Regs., Part II. and the Staff Manual respectively. Title pages will be prepared in manuscript.

WAR DIARY
or
INTELLIGENCE SUMMARY.
(Erase heading not required.)

Army Form C. 2118.

Place	Date	Hour	Summary of Events and Information	Remarks and references to Appendices
Lenze	1/4/19 -30/4/19		2/4/19. Lt. T O Balk. assumed command of the Company vice Capt V J Hook posted to the Army of the Rhine	
			11/4/19 Authority received to demobilise 30% of cadre personnel	
			No other events worthy of record occurred.	
			T O Balk Lt OC 52 Div Eng Coy R.E.	

D. D. & L., London, E.C.
(A10266) Wt W5300/P713 750,000 2/18 Sch. 52 Forms/C2118/16.

58 D. Signals

VOL 58

30

Army Form C. 2118.

Instructions regarding War Diaries and Intelligence Summaries are contained in F. S. Regs., Part II. and the Staff Manual respectively. Title pages will be prepared in manuscript.

WAR DIARY
or
INTELLIGENCE SUMMARY.

(Erase heading not required.)

Place	Date	Hour	Summary of Events and Information	Remarks and references to Appendices
Leuze	2/6/19	10.01	Signal Offices at Reboeil (291 Bde R.F.A.), Blicquy (290 Bde R.F.A.) and Ellignies (Div. Sub-Exchange) closed	Censor
	3/6/19		290 Bde R.F.A. moved to Leuze.	
	15/6/19		Signal Office closed: Cadre & Equipment Guard entrained for Antwerp.	
	16/6/19		Cadre & Equipment Guard arrived at Antwerp & marched to Base Camp	
	20/6/19		Vehicles & Equipment loaded on barges	
	22/6/19		Cadre & Equipment Guard entrained for Boulogne	
	23/6/19		Cadre & Equipment Guard arrived at Boulogne & marched to Demob. Camp	
	25/6/19		" " " embarked for U.K.	

[illegible]
Lt. 58 Div. Sig. Coy. R.E.

D. D. & L., London, E.C.
(A10266) Wt W5300/P713 750,000 2/18 Sch. 52 Forms/C2118/16.

www.ingramcontent.com/pod-product-compliance
Lightning Source LLC
Chambersburg PA
CBHW081421160426
43193CB00013B/2166
* 9 7 8 1 4 7 4 5 3 1 1 0 8 *